BRAIN SMART

HOW TO REGAIN FOCUS, MANAGE DISTRACTIONS, AND ACHIEVE MORE

Dr. Jenny Brockis

MARRI
PRESS

Brain Smart!

How To Regain Focus, Manage Distractions, And Achieve More

Dr. Jenny Brockis, MB ChB FRACGP

Published November 2013

Layout by Renée Fulton

Design and illustrations by Renée Fulton

Edited by Jem Bates

ISBN 978-0-9871475-4-7

Copyright © Dr.Jenny Brockis 2013

A CIP catalogue of this book is available from the National Library of Australia

Other than for review, private study or research as allowed by the Copyright Act no part of this book may be reproduced, copied, scanned, stored in a retrieval system, recorded or transmitted by any means or in any form without the written permission of the publisher.

Disclaimer: The information in this book is of a general nature only and does not constitute medical advice. It is not intended to replace the services of a doctor. Concerning the information contained in this book, readers should consult their own medical or health practitioner in regard to their own individual circumstances and needs.

The author, publisher and editor disclaim all responsibilities and liabilities to any person, arising directly or indirectly from either taking action or not taking action based on the information in this publication.

For John

ACKNOWLEDGEMENTS

I learned so much from putting together the first book in this series, *Brain Fit*. Not least I discovered a love and appreciation for stories, for words and language, and for the research that provides us with the understanding we have today about our marvelous brain. It was a truly collaborative effort, and this book has been no different.

My family have become accustomed to Mum spending many hours typing away in her study. They have understood, and tolerated, that dinner is sometimes a bit late and that she isn't always available at the right time to help them with their needs (although she's working hard on that one!).

As always, my friends have been totally supportive and encouraging, even though they think I must be a little crazy. I have also had the most amazing support from my mentors and speaking colleagues – Jason Fox and Matt Church, thank you for believing in me, challenging me, and keeping me accountable.

It is the team behind the book who make it possible. My profound thanks go to Jem Bates, editor; Geraldine Blake, proofreader; and Renée Fulton for the graphics and layout. Thanks guys.

PREFACE

After writing my first book, *Brain Fit*, I thought that would be it. Done and dusted. A publication on the shelf to accompany my work in the area of brain fitness, showing people how to incorporate those lifestyle choices that allow us to conserve and maintain optimal brain health and function.

What I noticed in my travels when delivering presentations and talking to people, though, was that not only were they hungry to find out more about their brain and how to preserve it for the longer term, they wanted something more. They wanted to know how to deal more effectively with everything else going on in their lives, such as how to keep up with the pace of life in general and how to continue to adapt to the rapid and steep trajectory of change we are currently experiencing.

I have heard many tales of stress and burnout, seen stress-related illness, broken relationships, failed marriages, loss of joie de vivre or a sense of what life is all about. This has contributed to my continuing quest for greater knowledge and understanding about our amazing brain, and has already taken me down the path of completing a Post Graduate Certificate in the Neuroscience of Leadership. My own insight has been that brain fitness is essentially the vital first step towards knowing what it takes to be able to use *your* brain to the best of *your* ability in everything you do, across your lifespan.

Working with our brain's wonderful natural plasticity, its ability to rewire itself in response to the sensory information it continually receives, means we can always continue to further develop and expand our brain's capacity to up-skill in those areas of brain function that we determine need a little more love and attention.

CONTENTS

PREFACE	v
INTRODUCTION	ix
1 JUST WHO IS IN THE CONTROL TOWER?	**1**
Paying attention to our attention	2
Introducing your executive suite: prima donna extraordinaire	4
Limited capacity: front row seats come at premium	4
Why working memory matters more than IQ	5
Energy saving by default: using your productive zone	7
Integrating circuits: the balance between instinct and reason	10
Why frazzle prevents dazzle	14
Keeping your brain safe at work	18
Refuel: focus requires fuel	21
Reinvigorate: exercise	22
Restore: sleep is paramount for focus	23
Tips for overcoming sleep deprivation	26
Fostering a nap-friendly workplace	27
2 DO WE STILL NEED MEMORY NOW THAT WE HAVE GOOGLE?	**30**
Why long-term memories are like catching fish	32
Why memory is flukey	35
Why remembering takes AGES	37
Bringing the class to attention	43
Attention changes the brain	44
Increasing attention density	45
Strengthening your attentional muscle	50
3 NOT DESIGNED FOR LONG-TERM FOCUS	**54**
Our shrinking attention span	59
Tips to help overcome ADT	61
Improving workload management	64
Why keeping a stiff upper lip doesn't help	66
Putting a different frame on things	67
Minding your mind – fully	70

4	MANAGING DISTRACTIONS AND MAKING THEM YOUR FRIENDS	74
	Knowing your enemies is crucial for survival	75
	The newest brain myth kid on the block: multitasking	78
	What's wrong with our brain?	83
	Multitasking stresses our brain	85
	Multitasking affects performance	88
	Taking back control of your inbox	90
	Why we love our social media	92
	The story so far about brains and technology addiction	92
	Tips to maintain phone and social media sanity	96
	Organisations and multitasking	100
	Avoiding multitasking in the workplace	103
	Can multitasking ever be trained?	106
5	PROCRASTINATE: WHY DO WE?	107
	What is procrastination?	109
	Hardwired to procrastinate	112
	Willpower: sharing our bucket of self-control	114
	Overcoming our procrastinating tendencies	116
	The paradox of too much choice	116
	Getting the value right	117
	Procrastination has all the elements of a good story	118
	Procrastination and getting started	118
	Procrastination and seeing things through	121
	Finishing off	124
	The value of deadlines	126
	Why it's not just about failing to plan	128
	Would you like to look at the dessert menu?	131
	Taming the beast of procrastination	134
6	BUILDING BRAIN SMARTNESS	138
	AFTERWORD: LIVING WITH A SMARTER BRAIN	140
	REFERENCES	141
	ABOUT THE AUTHOR	148

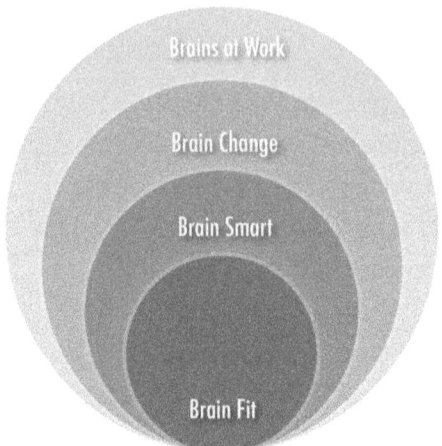

BRAIN FIT

Builds the foundation for optimal brain health and function to provide balance, wellbeing and performance.

BRAIN SMART

Creates awareness of how to regain focus, manage distractions, and boost productivity.

BRAIN CHANGE

Develops a framework for greater contribution and collaboration to adapt seamlessly to the ever-changing needs of our world.

BRAINS AT WORK

Examines work culture and asks the questions about the "how" and "why" we work, and what is required to make our work meaningful.

Brain Smart is the second in a series of books that explores the science behind *why* we think and behave the way we do, and *how* we can use this knowledge in practical ways to help us live more effectively and productively and enjoy happier, more fulfilled lives.

My hope is that this series will provide useful and practical applications for everyone who chooses, as suggested by Santiago Ramón y Cajal, to become better sculptors of their own brain.

INTRODUCTION

Describing someone as "smart" often implies that they are naturally intelligent, a problem solver, intuitive, insightful, innovative and good at business. So is such an interpretation accurate, or just wishful thinking?

Being a smart thinker can help us enormously in everyday life, whether at work or with simple challenges such as knowing how to get from A to B. In the classic 1960s American TV series *Get Smart*, hapless secret agent Maxwell Smart battles to foil the evil KAOS's plans to take over the world. Contrary to Max's hilarious incompetence, being smart generally implies you have the nous to use your brain effectively to solve problems and to overcome adversity more easily. It also implies that you have the capacity to expand beyond your current position, no matter where you are right now on life's ladder.

Yet not everyone necessarily sees being smart as a good thing. It can provoke jealousy, envy and fear. Being the smart kid at school, for example, can be a blessing or a curse. If your teacher thinks you are smart, you may be shown favour, and be encouraged to expand your knowledge and study to develop academically, because you are seen to be "clever". Your peers, however, may have a different viewpoint, seeing you as the nerdy "Goody Two Shoes" who receives unfair advantage and who therefore deserves to be picked on or bullied.

So how can we embrace our smartness, our natural cleverness, to build our brains to everyone's advantage, and why would this be a good idea?

In his book *Five Minds for the Future*[1], Howard Gardner, Professor of Cognition and Education, talks about the need to apply our smarts, our multiple intelligences, across the domains of discipline, synthesis, creativity, respect and ethics to enable us to achieve a higher level of success in life and work, and to survive and adapt well to the ever-changing needs of our highly complex and challenging world.

It can be easy to recognise the person with either great interpersonal skill or intuition or creativity or analytical competence. None of these is necessarily better than any another. Perhaps the question we could be asking, however, is how can we interweave these strengths so as to synergise and elevate our mental capacity — for example, by being great at processing information quickly, and at interpersonal relationships.

This book introduces ideas that can help you to develop your own smartness, as well as an understanding of why our brain sometimes lets us down — why we sometimes forget things that matter to us; why we go blank when standing up to present in front of others; and why we may find ourselves at the wrong destination, wondering, "How did I get here?" and "Why do I allow myself to get side-tracked when I know I ought to be doing something else?"

The book *Brain Fit*[2] covered the "how to" to help you build your level of brain fitness through better lifestyle choices. This provides a foundation and framework to enable you to produce a more optimised and healthy brain that can build in more cleverness.

Today our brains encounter many new and complex challenges. Happily, the latest brain science can help us understand both what works best to survive the challenges we confront, and also how to continue to adapt and use our brain to keep up with the rapid trajectory of change.

Brain Smart will show you what it takes to regain focus and remember more, to effectively manage the distractions that can cause so much frustration, to procrastinate less, and to increase your brain's resilience for dealing with those curve balls in life that threaten to knock you off target.

Whatever your starting point, building smartness begins with self-awareness, the intent to up-skill, and the perseverance to see it through.

If you could achieve all these things and enjoy the benefit of higher levels of performance and balance, what difference would it make to your life right now?

What Is Happening In Today's Workplace?

In recent years there have been many changes in the workplace, in how we do our work and in where we do our work. These changes have been accompanied by a shift in the expectations we set ourselves, as well as what others may expect of us. Such expectations are often based on our perception of what our "real" world is — a perception based on assumptions, and coloured by our beliefs and biases, which may not be shared by others.

What are some of the common statements you hear about the workplace today?

Here are some of the ones I encounter most often. What are your thoughts about these? Do you agree or disagree? (Later in the book, I'll explain why we might be thinking this way, and the brain science that can be used to help us overcome some of the associated difficulties.)

We are all so busy.

The modern workplace is busy, demanding, and often downright exhausting. When I ask people what they have noticed about the way they work, or what they think about the demands of their work, they all tell the same story. It doesn't matter if you are the CEO, a manager, a staff member, a student, or even a retiree, everyone says they are constantly busy, with too much to do and never enough time to do it in.

All this busyness can of course be alluring. If you are busy, you must be getting a lot done, your work must be terribly important and you must be very efficient. Yet is this an illusion? Are we this busy because we have overloaded our brains with too much to do in too little time, or are we simply creating additional work for ourselves?

I've heard the advice many times: If you have something that must be done, give it to a busy person. Good grief, what did that poor person do to deserve this attention? Is it because they don't know how to say no, or because they already have so much to do that you think they won't feel the pain of yet more work and they'll just slot in that extra task somewhere? Or is it because you assume that, despite knowing they already have too much to do, they still have the capacity and ability to get it done?

Have we in fact adapted to a state of perpetual busyness as being the social norm that makes not being busy no longer socially acceptable?

- Are you busy because you want to be, or because you fear not being busy?
- Is your busyness distracting you from what you really need to be paying attention to?
- Could you in fact be addicted to this busyness and costing yourself time, money and performance?

We have an increasing workload.

I have heard it frequently commented on that the complexity of our work tasks has increased along with the amount of personal responsibility assumed for getting the work done. Have you ever had the experience of the job description not actually matching your boss's expectations for what your new role really entails?

Our new technology is meant to be labour saving, allowing us to get on with other important aspects of our job such as planning and innovating. Yet how many times do you find yourself having to work harder or stay late because the technology has failed — a photocopier jams, the internal server goes down, or your smart phone goes on the blink?

Staff turnover, training days, sickness, holidays and budget cuts all affect who is available to do the work at any particular time.

- Is your work more complex than it used to be?
- Do you have to juggle many more tasks or projects at one time?
- Do you find yourself relying increasingly on the input of others and their ability to manage their workloads effectively to produce a piece of work?

We are all short of time.

A common perception many of us seem to share is that we have become time poor. It's as though the amount of time available to us in any 24-hour period has been squeezed into an ever-smaller shoebox. Rationally, we know that the number of hours and minutes available is the same, but our experience is that we always seem to be running out of time to meet the next deadline, to submit a tender, or to complete an assignment. Meanwhile, the next items requiring our attention and the ones after that are lining up, waiting their turn.

How much work have you got waiting in the wings, reminding you that there will be no letup just because you finish what you are currently working on?

- Do you share this perception of time poverty?

- Do you start your day thinking if only I could squeeze in another couple of hours?
- How would life look different to you if you could shift from feeling time poor to time abundant?

We are all working longer.

Within the workplace, have you noticed a shift in how much time we are expected to work? Perhaps you remember the era when the office workday was strictly from 9 am to 5 pm, with perhaps an hour for lunch and short breaks for morning and afternoon tea. When was the last time you enjoyed your full lunch break, or even had the luxury of getting one at all? How many times have you either skipped lunch because you were too busy, or grabbed something quick that you could eat in front of your computer?

As a student on summer vacation, I once worked in a factory that made paper products. My role? I was in the canteen making hundreds of "bacon butties" and giant urns of stewed tea for the morning and afternoon tea breaks. Large trolleys dripping fat and sugary confections were pushed around the offices of busy and hungry workers with the catch-cry "Wiv or wivout?" — referring to whether or not you took sugar in your tea, of course.

Some workplaces have recognised that eating at your desk is not healthy and have banned the practice. Studies have revealed that keyboards are a major source of bacteria so this is good from a health and safety perspective, but it fails to address the basic problem of getting brains to take a well-deserved break at lunchtime, so as to provide the required energy and capacity for the rest of the day. Perhaps there is a place for the tea trolley to return to the workplace to provide a welcome "brain break" and refuelling stop.

Cultural expectations in some workplaces have so evolved that you demonstrate your loyalty and commitment to your team or organisation by coming in early and/or staying late. Leaving work on time or, heaven forbid, early because you have a medical appointment, or because you want to attend your child's athletic/drama/music event is often frowned upon and seen as a quick way to sabotage your career prospects. This pervasive 'badge of honour' is sneaky because it is not usually written into contracts. You just learn that that's the way things are done, and if you want to stick around you'd better be seen to conform.

That's not to say that wanting to contribute more to your workplace is bad. Far from it. Indeed, many workplace cultures are moving towards far greater individual input, recognising that this creates a sense of meaning to the work being done, and a very powerful motivator to enhance collaboration and productivity.

What isn't healthy from the brain's perspective, is the unspoken expectation of having to stay behind or take on extra work, simply because "that is the way things are done".

- If you stay late, or get to work early, is it because you simply love your work, or because you feel there is always more to be done?
- Is overtime something you do for the money, or as a way of keeping up?
- If you are spending longer at work, or undertaking work-related tasks, how are you allocating time to your other roles in life?

We always have to continue to strive.

Another expectation that appears to have crept into the work culture, is that regardless of your current position, you always have to be seen to be striving to get to the next level, even when you are at the top. Being the best in your team or department is just a stepping-stone to the expected promotion, bonus or pay rise. If your personality is very self-driven, this may seem the natural thing to be doing. How often do we continue to drive ourselves on because of the expectations of others? This constant drive can have many sources, including partners, family and friends, in addition to work colleagues. No one likes to be seen as a "failure" or as someone who lets others down, so we push on, always giving our very best, striving for that new job or position, not necessarily because we are suited to it or even want it, but because it's the expected thing to do.

- Have you ever found yourself applying for a job or position you didn't want because it was expected of you?
- Have you ever turned down a promotion or job opportunity because you recognised it was beyond your level of competence?
- Have you ever found yourself encouraging someone else, whom you see as having great potential, to step up, without first checking that it's what they really want to do?

We have to ensure our survival.

Across the course of our evolution, human beings have demonstrated their capacity to adapt and survive. In the modern workplace having a job for life is no longer the norm. People change jobs, positions and roles frequently. There is often a desire to do this, especially on the part of the businesses and organisations ever mindful of the need to manage budgets, and only keep the best or right people for a particular project. It helps them to weed out those they don't wish to keep, and can help to lower presenteeism (where an employee is disengaged and fails to contribute to their best ability).

The downside of this for the individual, however, is that this change of job culture has also led to greater levels of insecurity and uncertainty where increasing numbers of staff are now employed on short-term contracts. Having to reapply for your position regularly is highly stressful as well as time-consuming. In some instances this has led to a culture in which, in order to survive and keep your job, you have to devise tactics and strategies to keep yourself one step ahead, because if you are seen to stumble there will likely be a stampede of others ready to take your place. This constant job insecurity can engender a culture of mistrust and self-interest.

- How safe do you feel in your job?
- Do you feel that your performance is under constant scrutiny, not so much to ensure you are continuing to grow professionally, but rather to ensure you are not making mistakes or failing to contribute?
- How much time and effort do you have to allocate to simply maintain your current role or position rather than work on your projects at hand?

We have information/communication overload.

Humans are very good at connecting and communicating with each other. Our social brains meant we devised ways to share knowledge and useful information that would be of benefit to others in our group.

Today, computers, the Internet, email, social media and smart phones allow us to connect with one another at a more intimate level in ways never previously imagined. However, this high level of interconnectivity and sharing of vast tracts of information has come at a cost to our cognition and wellbeing.

A great deal of recent research indicates that our need to stay connected is causing some people problems in switching off.

We are seeing increasing numbers of people being treated for addiction problems in relation to technology, whether it is email or smart phones or video games.

- Do you ever have trouble switching off or "disconnecting" from work?
- Do you take your smart phone/tablet/laptop away with you on holiday "to stay in touch"?
- Do you ever worry about how much time you spend online?

We lack sufficient data filters.

Having access to information today is like living in Aladdin's cave. There is so much information available we are drowning in it, and it's not just a problem in the workplace; it affects students too.

The need for knowledge experts is diminishing because everyone can now access all the knowledge they need (and far more) with just a few keystrokes. So the issue is no longer difficulty in accessing the information; it's about knowing how to filter the information, to distinguish what is relevant and accurate from what is off topic or unreliable.

Without adequate filters, students (and workers) can become paralysed by the amount of information to be sorted, so increasingly they focus on skimming large volumes of information. This trend concerns many educators, who see that as a consequence we cover a far broader field of information but at ever less depth. Skimmed information means our brains have insufficient data to gain real meaning and understanding of the subject being studied.

Then, of course, it is about knowing what to do with all this information once acquired. With the drive towards the paperless office, workplaces require increasingly sophisticated ways to store and cross-reference data so it is not simply lost. Recognising this problem, some organisations and businesses have assigned Chief

Data Officers whose role is to manage the information effectively. Smaller organisations have had to rely on more traditional storage methods while new software support packages are introduced.

- Do you have a love–hate relationship with your inbox?
- Do you sometimes wish technology could automatically filter only what you need and advise what is relevant at this present time?
- Do you ever wish you could go back to a time when you worked harder to acquire less but better information?

We lack upgrade managers.

This leads to the next challenge: updates. Your computer will automatically send you the regular software updates needed for you to continue to use the system effectively. Then there is the hardware itself. Apple, Samsung and Microsoft are constantly looking for new ways to upgrade their products. The demand is always there, with innovators and early up-takers queuing to be first to purchase the latest smart phone or tablet.

A new computer today, while not as expensive as it was ten years ago, isn't going to last any longer — quite the opposite. A computer is now considered obsolescent and requiring replacement within three to five years because of the continuing release of new and much more powerful processors, memory and graphics, which means our technical capability is rapidly outstripping our capacity to keep up in many areas.

So what about the human brain? Keeping up with new ideas and technology requires our brain to adapt and rewire itself at an ever faster rate. We have so many apps to inform, educate and entertain us, how can our brain stay focused and attentive for long enough to take in and adapt to the next round of upgrades?

- Do you ever worry that your brain simply can't keep up with the rapid pace of change?
- Do you ever wish you could find an app that would allow your brain to upgrade automatically?
- Do you resist technological change by choosing not to upgrade, and opting out of the conversation?

We have a widening generation brain gap.

Much has always been made of the generation gap and the challenges it can pose. In today's workplace, it is not the differences in hairstyles or fashion or music tastes, but the "brain gap" that is most pronounced. Young brains are wired differently. The Millennials,[3] as "digital natives", have grown up only knowing a digital world, with no experience of a time before the Internet or mobile phones.

This widening brain gap can manifest itself in the way we communicate and interact with different generations. We need not pass judgement on these differences, but they do need to be acknowledged so we can discover the best ways for all brains to work successfully together. Millennials are different from previous generations in that their neuronal wiring makes them capable of handling multiple tasks better, despite having a shorter attention span.

- Have you ever had an intergenerational brain clash?
- Have you ever caught yourself thinking negative thoughts about the capacity of brains of a different generation from yourself?
- Have you or your workplace considered how to close the brain gap by getting all brains to collaborate more effectively together?

We lack a brain-safe and brain-friendly workplace.

One very significant challenge for the workplace today is staying brain fit. Occupational Health and Safety has focused on securing the physical wellbeing of workers in the workplace. However, there is much work to be done to ensure the modern workplace is a safe place for all brains.

The incidence of depression is escalating rapidly in society. It is now the leading cause of disability in the workplace. One in five Australians[4] will experience an episode of mental illness in any given year, and that accounts only for those cases reported. Recognising the factors that contribute to an individual's risk of developing mental illness, whether related to stress, anxiety, depression or psychosis, remains an underfunded area that receives too little attention.

Is this because there is still a stigma attached? Is there a state of denial about the extent to which mental illness affects the workplace, or is it seen as too problematic or too uncomfortable a topic to draw attention to? The reality is that ignoring it won't make it go away, and the cost to the individual, their family, the workplace and society is huge.

The cost of presenteeism[5] in the Australian workplace in 2010 was $34.1 billion, four times the cost of absenteeism and equivalent to 2.7% of Australia's GDP. Presenteeism is the face of the person who makes it to work, and indeed often works long hours, but fails to be engaged in the work and struggles to be productive. Financial worries, health issues, relationship difficulties, or other problems can have a significant impact on our ability to work and to work well.

- Have you witnessed or experienced mental distress in your workplace?

- What policy has your workplace adopted to ensure that all employees are brain fit as well as physically fit?
- If no policy is currently in place, what could you be doing to ensure that all brains share the same advantage of knowing how to work smarter and safer?

In light of these challenges, which affect many of us to a greater or lesser degree, what can the new brain science do to help us overcome or at least manage them better?

Let's take a look.

CHAPTER 1

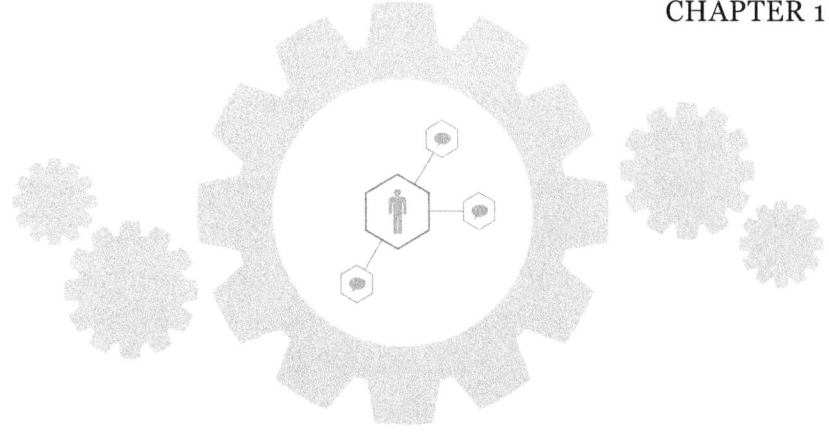

JUST WHO IS IN THE CONTROL TOWER?

We developed our ability to pay focused attention principally as a survival tool. It was important to be able to focus on where food could be found, where there was a safe place to sleep, and of course to find a mate. In other words, we needed attention to know that we were safe, that we could find and utilise this great food source, and by the way, I really like you and want to have your babies. Our needs were, and remain, fairly simple really!

Paying attention has allowed us to survive while maintaining our awareness of what was going on around us. Being totally engrossed in a good book can be highly enjoyable but it is important that we can still respond if someone speaks to us, the doorbell rings, or a fire breaks out.

Paying attention is crucial for us to be able to learn. It is part of the process our brain uses to form memory by engaging our prefrontal cortices in our frontal lobes and the part of the brain called the hippocampus, an area intricately involved in learning and memory.

PAYING ATTENTION TO OUR ATTENTION

Pete was in the middle of writing a complex Excel spreadsheet when Geoff, one of his team coordinators, knocked on his door and asked if he could have a quick word. Without taking his attention away from his spreadsheet, Pete answered, "Sure, fire away". Geoff expressed his concern about another member of the team, Paul, who he thought was struggling with his current workload, and wondered if Pete could have a chat with him to check if everything was okay. While Geoff was still talking, Pete's PA called him to advise there was an urgent phone call from a major client.

Three weeks later, Pete heard that Paul had been admitted to hospital with severe depression and was likely to be off work for some time. Paul was a competent and valuable member of Pete's team. Pete thought very highly of him and was very surprised by the news. He wondered what could have brought on his illness — and then he remembered Geoff's warning, which he had forgotten all about and taken no action on.

In our busy world we are all rushing around so fast trying to complete all our tasks that we don't always allow our brains the time and the environment it needs to focus, and focus deeply on what really matters.

Molecular biologist John Medina, in his book *Brain Rules*[6], writes, "The brain does not pay attention to boring things".I don't know how many of us allow ourselves the luxury of being bored any more, but I have spoken to many people who find they don't have the time or energy to devote to some of the important things that do matter, such as:

- Spending time with family and friends to chill out and relax
- Talking about current affairs, a movie or a book

- Allocating enough time to fulfil all the requirements ahead of a looming deadline
- Scheduling that doctor's appointment for a routine check-up.

Because we are all so busy, we spend much of our time skimming the surface of our activities, or worse, lose sight of our target. Students will often spend hours on the Internet looking for relevant information for an assignment, and then find themselves side-tracked to sites that are completely off topic.

Our ability to pay attention is defined as the brain's capacity to focus on the task at hand while actively inhibiting all distractions. If only it was that simple!

INTRODUCING YOUR EXECUTIVE SUITE: PRIMA DONNA EXTRAORDINAIRE

The human brain has been quietly evolving for thousands of years. One of the greatest advances in that development has been the acquisition of our magnificent frontal lobes, our neocortex.

This relatively new part of the brain allows us to think about our thinking. It is our conscious thought. It provides us with the means to regulate another, older part of our brain, the limbic system, which has always kept us safe but lacks the finesse of the frontal lobes which are aptly called our executive suite: to plan, organise, apply the brain's emotional brakes and operate our working memory.

The neocortex is also quite the "prima donna" in that, like Goldilocks, it likes everything to be "just right" and is highly influenced by a number of different factors.[7] The smooth operation of the frontal lobes is often at the mercy of our neurochemicals, hormones and the limbic system, which is always seeking to gain control. This can be an ongoing challenge in an ever-changing environment with multiple variables.

Our frontal lobes operate more slowly than the limbic system. It takes time to pause, reflect, and compare and contrast other information, memories and experiences, which is why in times of emergency it is our limbic system that jumps in first to get us out of harm's way.

LIMITED CAPACITY: FRONT SEATS COME AT A PREMIUM

Our working memory — what used to be known as short-term memory — is located in the prefrontal cortex, part of the frontal lobes, and it works in rather cramped conditions in a very small area. Maybe the next remodelling of our brain will bring an upgrade, but until then we have to work with the system that is available. This essentially means we can hold an average of seven different items (plus or minus two) in our working memory at any one time, though if the concepts are more complex or if the brain is older, this is reduced to three or four.

Though when it comes to focusing attention, the space available becomes even more restricted: we can focus on only one item at any given time. This sometimes causes a bottleneck, with new ideas in a holding pattern, waiting to find a bit of space to be considered.

Hence it is essential to provide the brain, and especially the energy-hungry prefrontal cortex, with a bit of breathing space. We were not designed to spend long periods of time focusing attention. It is cognitively exhausting and costs the brain too much in terms of mental energy. Providing the brain with soothing interludes gives us the tea break we all need to relax and stretch our cognitive legs.

So when you face a particularly challenging mental task, it pays to get in early while your brain is still fresh, and to provide the prefrontal cortex with enough time and energy to deal with the issue effectively.

WHY WORKING MEMORY MATTERS MORE THAN IQ

In the modern workplace, where time is of the essence, our mental flexibility and ability to work quickly with information is a crucial skill.

Our working memory resides in the frontal lobes. What differentiates working memory from long-term memory is that working memory allows us to manipulate information in the short term, whether it is a telephone number, a PIN, the address of a work colleague, or the items we mean to buy in the supermarket.

Some neuroscientists believe that our working memory is a stronger indicator of intelligence than academic intelligence, because the ability to maintain an agile and flexible working memory is seen as a cognitive advantage that is more significant for actual success. Since the introduction of working memory training programs, though, the jury remains out on whether such training imparts a significant biological advantage, or merely makes us more adept at handling some pieces of information in the short term.

Torkel Klingberg[8], of the Karolinska Institute, author of *The Overflowing Brain*, has devised his own working memory training program called Cogmed, aimed at assisting children diagnosed with ADD or ADHD. This type of working memory training is now being investigated to

> Some neuroscientists believe that our working memory is a stronger indicator of intelligence than academic intelligence.

see how it might usefully be applied to helping people of all ages with attentional deficits.

In the education system, many students identified with various types of learning disability have appeared to gain benefit from participating in programs such as the Fast ForWord Program, which is part of Sonic Learning.

Incidentally, we now use the term *working memory* instead of short-term memory because it is recognised to be an active process, although Mark Katz[9], a child psychologist from San Diego, suggests the term *working attention* might be an even better descriptor.

ENERGY SAVING BY DEFAULT: USING YOUR PRODUCTIVE ZONE

With this focus on how to pay better attention and manage distractions, it's easy to think that that's all we should be concentrating on. However, in reality the brain doesn't like to remain focused for too long. It uses up too much brain energy and, being an energy-conscious organ, it has its own way of ensuring we don't burn up too much mental fuel. It does this by reverting to its default system,[10] thereby imposing its own brain breaks.

How long can you stay focused on a task? If you have ever experienced being 'in the flow', you'll know that glorious state when time simply melts away and you experience total concentration and full engagement on your task, which seems to come together almost magically. It is a truly joyful feeling, but not one that many of us get to taste that often.

Our normal attention span is around 10–12 minutes at best, but more often closer to five minutes. Which means that to stay engaged with a particular task we have to refocus our attention actively and frequently.

OUR NORMAL ATTENTION SPAN IS AROUND 10-12 MINUTES AT BEST, BUT MORE OFTEN CLOSER TO FIVE MINUTES.

Louise is a primary school teacher who knows only too well how important it is to keep her charges' attention. She has devised her lessons so that every ten minutes or so she re-engages the class by asking a question, or asking her students to look at a picture, watch a video clip, or participate in a group activity. Providing their brains with new stimuli relating to the material ensures that her students stay focused, and hence more likely to retain the information they are learning.

As adults we learn in exactly the same way. So how do you re-engage your brain at work to stay focused?

Your brain has an optimum time for learning. Cognitively as adults, we are set up to be most alert from around 6 am, when we wake up, peaking at 10 am, so many people use the first few hours of their working day to get their really important work done. Teenagers, being a separate species, actually have a different brain clock for learning and sleeping. They learn more effectively starting later in the day.

Your brain uses more than 400 different neurotransmitters, hormones and enzymes to function normally. One of these neurotransmitters is called acetylcholine (ACH) and is essential for learning. It too has a couple of peaks and troughs during the day. Knowing how to work with your brain allows you to get the most out of your day.

So if you have a lot of things to do, try scheduling your tasks so you do the most important ones first, and write up your schedule for the next day, the night before. This is a really good way to make your days more productive, especially if you have really long to-do lists.

For students wondering how best to structure their study time, working with your brain means working for regulated periods of time, preferably of around 45 minutes to 90 minutes maximum, and then enjoying a well-earned brain break of 10 to 15 minutes doing something *completely unrelated* to the previous activity. Far from being time wasted, these brain breaks ensure your brain stays focused and recharged for longer, and help you retain the information more effectively.

You may have recognised that you have your own unique productive zone, that time when you are at your most engaged and productive. For many people that is in the morning. Morning people like to get up early and get a few things ticked off their to-do list, preferably before the start of the working day, enjoying an exercise or meditation session, completing a household task, or even just doing some important thinking related to their studies or work, because they know this is the time when their brain is switched to maximum thinking power.

Others of us are night workers. Mornings are not our scene, until after at least our third cup of double shot espresso, but as the day progresses our productive levels start to ramp up. Later, when the larks are all safely tucked up in bed, the owls are coming out to play hard.

Still others of us sit squarely in the middle. Whether you are a morning person, a night time worker, or someone who sits in the middle doesn't matter. It's all about recognising when you work best with your brain.

Some people assume that daydreaming is a bad thing. At school kids are often told off for daydreaming, but teachers could be doing their students a disservice. Scientists have discovered that daydreaming is often a time when the brain is using our subconscious to help resolve a problem or challenge. Of course, too much daydreaming means the task at hand is not being attended to so, as in all things, it's all about finding the happy medium.

For everyone the challenge, though, is the same. We have only two to three hours a day of really good focused time. So use your best thinking time wisely.

INTEGRATING CIRCUITS: THE BALANCE BETWEEN INSTINCT AND REASON

The prefrontal cortex has its work cut out with all the "harder" aspects of thinking.

Meanwhile, your subconscious brain has been anything but idle.

One way the brain devised to conserve precious mental energy was to habituate certain tasks or activities. These are our habits. We form habits because these are the tasks we do most often and require little cognitive energy to make them happen. How much focused time do you really need to spend getting dressed, opening the fridge door, or having a shower? Okay, I know that we girls sometimes spend some focused attention time choosing which clothes to wear, but once selected we use automatic behaviour to put the clothes on. This is good, because it frees up mental energy for the prefrontal cortex to devote to other, harder cognitive tasks such as organising new information and manipulating it to be useful to us.

Our neocortex is the baby of the brain in evolutionary terms. It has been the last part of our brain to evolve, and is the last part to mature (around our mid twenties). It is very demanding and comparatively slow. It takes time to pause and reflect, compare and contrast, and consider all options.

The limbic system is far older. It evolved very early on and is shared by all other creatures with brains. Our limbic system keeps us safe, recognising if we are in danger and alerting the stress response of fight, flee or freeze. It is also very fast, which is ideal as you don't want to be hanging about trying to decide what is the best plan of action while a big truck is bearing down and about to run you over. Our limbic system gathers information pertinent to our surroundings, which forms our emotions, which we then bring to our level of consciousness as feelings.

Expressing our feelings allows us to communicate the emotions we are experiencing. Our facial expressions transmit whether we are happy or sad, anxious or curious. To keep us safe, the brain is constantly scanning our environment for signs of danger. We have a default system too, which essentially means our brain first assumes anything new or different is potentially dangerous, and asks questions later.

Amanda noticed with alarm that she had a ladder in her new tights. How did that happen? She was sitting on a plastic-coated chair in the stuffy waiting area with seven other people who all looked as hot and uncomfortable as she felt.

The job advert had looked really appealing when she first saw it, but now, waiting her turn to go before the interview panel, she wondered why she had ever thought that. Looking at everyone else also waiting, she decided they all looked far superior to her and much more likely to be selected for the position. It probably wasn't too late to walk nonchalantly to the door and leave . . . and then she heard her name being called.

When we are in a new situation, such as a job interview, starting a new job or meeting a new colleague, we can feel apprehensive. Our amygdala, which is part of the limbic system, is on high alert for cues to determine whether we should stay or run.

Our instinct may keep us safe, but we need our slower, more ponderous prefrontal cortex to evaluate all the pros and cons to help us decide what is the reality, even though our instinct made up its mind well before. That rustle in the grass may indeed be a tiger waiting to sink his fangs into you, but it could also simply be a wind gust. The prefrontal cortex and limbic region play a delicate dance of balance, but one in which the amygdala and rest of the limbic system desperately want to take the lead if given even the hint of opportunity.

Under normal circumstances your prefrontal cortex can down-regulate or up-regulate the limbic response. Though if your brain has been subjected to severe or chronic stress, that ongoing stimulus leads to a hyper-alert and hyper-stimulated amygdala. Eventually your exhausted brain reaches a critical point, stress hormones are at a maximum, and the amygdala succeeds in forcing the prefrontal cortex to relinquish control.

We now have an amygdala "hijack".[11] This is when we lose our brain's brakes and operate entirely on emotion. When you are having a huge argument, for example, you may then say things, or act in a way that is way out of character, because you no longer have the influence of your prefrontal cortex to calm things down. This is why you see highly intelligent, articulate, smart people sometimes making really bad judgement calls. Unable to access previous memory or experience in your super-stressed state, unable to take in new information, your brain becomes effectively deaf, dumb, and blind.

Making the wrong choice in relation to picking the new colour for your office walls is one thing, but what if as CEO your extreme stress levels are influencing all of your decision making and problem solving?

Too much stress can cause you to:
- **Misinterpret the information at hand**
- **Experience a loss of concentration and focus**
- **Become unable to follow instructions**
- **Be less likely to take necessary precautions**

 ## BEING EXPOSED TO CHRONIC STRESS MAKES US BELIEVE THIS IS OUR "NORMAL", WHEN IT IS ANYTHING BUT.

In July 2005, following the bombings in central London, armed police wrestled a man to the floor of an Underground train and shot him repeatedly in the head, believing his demeanour matched that of a potential terrorist. He was an unarmed student from Brazil.

In the aftermath of the 9/11 disaster, it came to light that some people in the Twin Towers died because they were unable to respond to the situation by looking for an exit. In their hyper-stressed state they froze to the spot.

The *Exxon Valdez* oil spill in 1989 resulted in between 260,000 and 750,000 barrels of oil being released into the Prince William Sound, Alaska, causing a major environmental disaster. Contributing factors included an exhausted and insufficient crew, and a third mate who failed to manoeuvre the tanker properly, or to use a radar system that could have warned of the impending disaster.

One problem of being exposed to too much stress over a prolonged period of time is that we get used to this being our "normal", when in fact it is anything but. Worse still, we fail to notice when the warning light on our brain's dashboard indicates that our stress levels have reached dangerously high levels, putting us at risk of imminent amygdala hijack and loss of prefrontal control.

It goes back to the children's story of the frog and the pot of water. If you toss a frog into a pot of boiling water, the frog is going to jump out pretty quickly because he recognises he is in danger. Yet if you put the frog into a pot of cool water and gently start heating it on the stove, the frog becomes used to the rising temperature and fails to jump out to save himself.

WHY FRAZZLE PREVENTS DAZZLE

Paying attention, learning new information, making decisions and solving problems are all in a day's work, and naturally we like to think it's our glorious thinking brain that is calling the shots. In reality, it is our subconscious brain that is determining our choices, our decisions and our actions.

We sometimes call this our "gut instinct" or intuition. It is actually our subconscious mind making decisions based on our previous experience and memories. Our subconscious is what influences and colours our perceptions and our interpretation of the world we experience. Sure, we can bring in our logical, rational, thinking brain too, but don't underestimate the power of the subconscious!

We make decisions in life and business all the time — an estimated 35,000 every day. That's a lot of decision making. They often have to be made quickly after weighing up all the information that is available to us, and they can be fraught with danger because a bad decision can cost money, time, or even lives. A decision that comes into the forefront of our consciousness, which we think we have come up with using our logical, rational, and analytical forebrain, was actually predetermined by our subconscious thoughts and driven by our emotion.

We make an estimated 35,000 decisions every day.

Teams that are working constantly under the pump of relentless, urgent deadlines never get the opportunity just to stop and reflect on the work completed and what needs to be done next. If everything is urgent because the client is demanding or the project is running late, the brain never gets any down time and remains in

 ## THE LOOK OF LOVE IS WHEN WE EXPERIENCE THAT EXTRA BIT OF STRESS IN THE NICEST POSSIBLE WAY

a hyper-vigilant and alert state that is cognitively exhausting and potentially damaging.

Simon was under immense pressure from his board to come up with a solution to a challenge that had been dogging his company for months. He had listened to various solutions proffered by his various teams and department heads, some of which had greater merit than others. He had narrowed down the choice to two: one offered a better long-term solution, but was very expensive and would take time to implement and to show results. It would also mean that some staff would have to be retrenched at a time when staff morale was already low. The other solution was a much cheaper "fix" that addressed the immediate problems without needing to sack staff, but which failed to provide an adequate framework for ongoing improvement and benefit to the company. He remained unsure of which would be the better path to follow.

Not only that, but Simon was in the middle of a messy divorce, one of his kids was having problems at school, and he had just heard that his mother had been diagnosed with a terminal illness.

One of the board members approached him with the news that a meeting was being called for 2 pm that afternoon, and Simon was expected to explain his position and his decision on which solution to go for at that time.

It is in this type of environment where executives, whilst being high achievers, often highly motivated and with a strong work ethic, can run into trouble with the unintended consequences presenting as burnout, high stress levels, and physical ill health.

The question that needs to be asked is, if "this is just business" or if "this is the way we do things around here" could this in fact could be potentially compromising productivity and performance because the brain is not designed to function at its best under these circumstances?

Poor decisions occur when our prefrontal cortex is under more stress than it can comfortably and effectively handle. It comes back again to balance, and the intricate interplay between the prefrontal cortex and the limbic system. In this instance, the main concern is to have in place a leader who doesn't just look good on paper but has the emotional intelligence skills in place, so that in a moment of crisis he or she can lead, and lead safely.

Stress per se is not a bad thing. It is a normal physiological response to your environment. You need stress not only to help get you out of bed in the morning; it also revs you up to anticipate the excitement or challenges the new day will bring. That's why our performance improves when we are first put under a little more pressure. We "step up" and improve our game.

When our level of stress rises, we experience a number of things in our body: a surge in the level of adrenalin accompanies an increased heart rate and breathing rate, and our pupils dilate. (The look of love is in fact a great example of a person who is experiencing that extra bit of stress in their system in the nicest possible way.) We become alert and we notice more in our environment, which is a good place to be on a Monday morning when starting your working week.

When studying for a test or exam, student performances rise as they prepare and rehearse the material they need to revise and learn. Medical students have been shown on brain scans to develop increased cortical density in those areas associated with the new learning, which sadly lasts only during the exam stress phase.

It's also a great place to be if you are engaged in a sport. Playing tennis, for example, you can successfully use that higher level of stress to observe your partner closely and stay focused, ready to play and win that next point.

Because every brain is different, every experience we have will be perceived and remembered in a unique way. How we respond and react to different stressors is unique to our brain. New technology fazes some people, the sight of blood stresses others, while some of us hate having to stand up and present in front of others. The emotion we experience with high levels of stress is often fear. How much we feel will vary from person to person, day to day, and event to event.

There is a tipping point, which varies from person to person and from circumstance to circumstance. A stress performance curve takes the shape of an inverted U, because at a certain point any additional stress causes the prefrontal cortex essentially to shut down and we are no longer able to access our logic, reasoning, or analysis of a particular situation.

How often do you hear "It's the last straw" when some relatively minor annoyance occurs, such as a child slamming a car door, or someone taking the parking bay you have just spent ten minutes waiting to move into. That's the time when the red mist can come down like a stage curtain and we "lose it".

This is why in some instances really intelligent people, often those in positions of authority or leadership, find themselves making some pretty lousy decisions, or behaving and speaking out of character. Their brains have simply reached the tipping point.

KEEPING YOUR BRAIN SAFE AT WORK

Understanding that your brain is constantly working hard to keep you safe helps us to recognise why we sometimes respond in a way which belies a more rational response.

Tim was at a lunchtime networking function. He was new to town and new to his position in the company, so he was keen to meet and get to know some of his other colleagues.

Having grabbed a plate of slightly curly-edged and tired-looking sandwiches, he scanned the room looking for someone to talk to. He spied a couple of people who were having a bit of a laugh and enjoying some sort of conversation. He walked across and introduced himself to Lewis and Gerald. Lewis responded instantly with a smile and a handshake. Tim felt at ease immediately, and glad that he had found someone he felt he could relate to.

WE DETERMINE WHETHER A PERSON THAT WE MEET IS FRIEND OR FOE IN ABOUT 1/5TH OF A SECOND.

Meanwhile, Gerald stood by, silent. Sensing his reticence, Tim tried to engage him, asking about his experience with the company, anything that would effectively break the ice. It didn't work, and within a couple of minutes Gerald excused himself and disappeared into the milling throng.

Tim was unsure what he had done wrong. He sensed that Gerald didn't like him and he wondered if it was his manner, or whether he had interrupted an important discussion.

We determine whether a person that we meet is friend or foe in about 1/5th of a second. Our subconscious has already made its judgement call even before we have opened our mouth to say hello, and our subconscious is heavily biased to the negative. Dr Evian Gordon[12], CEO of the Brain Resource Company, explains that our brain works in one of two ways. We are looking either to minimise danger, in which case we want to move away. Or we look to receive a reward, in which case we demonstrate a "towards" response. Our bias is towards the negative because it makes sense that in order to stay safe we assume the worst first, and ask questions later.

Tim had created an "away" response in the other person's mind. What he didn't know was that Tim bore a resemblance to another person that Gerald had previously worked with, and with whom he had had a personality clash. Through no fault of his own, other than to look a bit like someone else, Tim had no chance currently to relate to Gerald. That would have to come later after a period of time in which Gerald would hopefully come to realise that Tim was actually very unlike the other person who had caused him grief.

So first impressions do count and are often heavily biased. The trouble is that once a negative view has been set up it takes much more effort and work to change our mind. That's because the "away" response is always much bigger, deeper and longer lasting than our "towards" response. We have to work a lot harder to earn our rewards, and when we do get them they are fairly fleeting by comparison.

Think back to when something went wrong for you. It could have been a reprimand for making a mistake, or it could have been something that someone said to you that felt hurtful or unkind. Your response to that may have been quite profound and long lasting. How many people do you know who carry their emotional "hurts" around with them, sometimes for years?

Conversely, now think of a time when you experienced something really rewarding: being acknowledged for great work done, receiving a pay rise or unexpected gift. The sense of reward you may feel is really good, but it doesn't last very long after that initial experience of elation and joy.

So it is really important when working with others to recognise that we all have our subconscious triggers that we are often unaware of and that will produce a response which, once determined, is very hard to change. If we can develop the skill of recognising how to minimise any potential threat response in ourselves as well as others, the possibility of raising the amount of reward experienced by everyone suddenly becomes a whole lot easier.

Looking for ways to minimise stress in our interactions on a daily basis goes back to understanding the importance of managing our own stress levels first, and then attending to others'. It's just like the safety advice we hear before take-off on a plane. In the event of an emergency, we are advised to ensure that we put our own oxygen mask on first before attending to our children. If we can't look after ourselves, we are not going to be of much use to anyone else.

In the workplace, and in life in general, it is possible to learn how to minimise the impact of stress on our thinking brain and maintain a better brain balance by regularly checking in on our stress loads and adjusting how much we are trying to cram into daily schedules.

For anyone who has had to live with or work with a prima donna, you have my commiserations. You will understand that in order to get the best performance out of them, it is imperative they are always provided with all the "essentials" that they deem critical to their ability to work at their best.

Your brain is no different, with a long list of 400 neurochemicals, hormones and enzymes to keep in balance, just the way your brain likes them to be. The trouble is, our brains are not only highly complex but inherently fragile and vulnerable to the differences in our environment, both internal and external.

In addition, it is vital that the basic commodities our brains require are also available to allow our brains to refuel, reinvigorate and restore as needed.

REFUEL: FOCUS REQUIRES FUEL

It goes without saying that our brain and our body rely heavily on having adequate fuel to perform at their best. If you have ever found yourself driving with the fuel gauge on empty, you'll know the uncomfortable, anxious experience of hoping you will make it to the nearest garage forecourt before the engine dies. Like cars, brains will cough, sputter, and stop running if they have insufficient fuel. Hunger is a stressor to your brain. It's much harder to concentrate when all you can think about is your growling stomach and how long it is until lunch. Our neurons do not store glucose, the brain's primary energy source, so it is essential that we stop for regular refuelling stops to take on board the appropriate food and water.

Our food choices also affect our brain's performance. Foods that are slow energy releasers are far better than those that cause a surge in sugar levels and then a crash and burn several hours later. That's why cheese and crackers are far better than a chocolate bar. Public health advocates have been promoting the message "Eat more fruit and vegetables" for over forty years. It is particularly important because they are great brain foods. Research has shown that a Mediterranean diet, which is based on fish (cold-water, oily types), green leafy vegetables, fruit (especially deeply pigmented berries), seeds, nuts, whole grains, and olive oil, is beneficial to good brain function, aiding memory and other thinking skills. They are also very important for long-term brain management, to keep your brain in tiptop shape over the longer term.

REINVIGORATE: GETTING BRAINS INTO SHAPE WITH EXERCISE

The role of exercise in our physical wellbeing has long been recognised. It is now very obvious from the available research that getting sufficient exercise is also critical to good brain function. We evolved to move, yet in today's world many of us now spend more time sitting than sleeping, and our sedentary nature is very bad for optimal brain function.

Some people try to overcome this lack of movement by working out several times a week. Unfortunately, this isn't enough to overcome the negative effect of all that sitting. We need to move more during our working day as well as exercising aerobically for between 30 and 60 minutes every day.

People who slot an exercise session into their daily routine before work have been shown to be more effective in their thinking and memory. They are mentally sharper, think with greater clarity, and have more energy to power through their day.

WE NEED TO MOVE MORE DURING OUR WORKING DAY AS WELL AS EXERCISING AEROBICALLY FOR BETWEEN 30 AND 60 MINUTES EVERY DAY.

In addition, the brain is stimulated by the exercise to produce higher amounts of certain neurochemicals including BDNF (brain derived neurotrophic factor), which not only enables a higher standard of maintenance of our existing neurons but stimulates neurogenesis. This is the process whereby the brain produces new neurons. Having a higher level of BDNF promotes the survival of the brain cells so they are more likely to reach maturity and be incorporated into our existing brain circuitry.

So next time you are having that inner dialogue with yourself about how you can justify not going to that exercise class, remind yourself: *your brain needs you to exercise!*

RESTORE: SLEEP IS PARAMOUNT FOR FOCUS

Suffice to say, sleep is probably one of the most essential requirements for good brain function. If we are to get really serious about how to ensure that we can pay attention when needed, to be able to form memory and recall what is important at the right time, we have to ensure we get enough sleep.

The one way to ensure you can lift performance and achieve more is by ensuring you get enough sleep. Period.

Yet today sleep is often treated as a being a bit of a nuisance. How many people do you know who try to reduce the amount of sleep they get in the false hope that this will enable them to get more done?

Wrong.

One of the challenges we face in today's society, especially when it comes to good brain health and function, relates to the amount of time we spend engaged with our new technology – both at work and in the home.

The potential health impact of the time we spend glued to our screens is beyond the scope of this book. Suffice to say that too much screen time can damage your health, particularly if you are a young child. The American Society of Paediatrics[13] is so concerned it has recommended that children under the age of two should not have *any* screen access because of the interfering effect it has on the developing brain for attentional, emotional, and socialisation skills. Yet how often do you see young children in their strollers

THE TROUBLE IS, AS SO MANY PEOPLE ARE CHRONICALLY SLEEP DEPRIVED, THEY HAVE PROBABLY FORGOTTEN WHAT IT'S LIKE TO HAVE A GOOD NIGHT'S SLEEP.

or out with their parents being entertained by a tablet computer?

Even having the TV on in a room where a child is playing has been shown to diminish the child's ability to stay on task with a favourite toy. Yet 30% of two- to five-year-olds already know how to operate a smart phone or tablet computer, and 61% can play a basic computer game. If a child is engaged in screen time, they are not going to be playing with other kids or going outside or be physically active, both crucial activities for normal brain development.

So what about grown-up brains? Does too much screen time harm your ability to perform at your best?

The demands of our work and study require many of us to spend time in the evenings to complete all our tasks. Time previously spent watching television is increasingly being spent on other forms of screen time, including your computer and smart phone.

The bluish light these screens emit can disrupt the brain's ability to recognise when it's time to sleep. Insomnia is a growing problem among people who complain of either not getting enough sleep or not getting quality sleep. The consequence is that many people are chronically sleep deprived and this leads to poorer work performance.

Losing a night's sleep has the same impact on your cognitive performance as driving drunk, and yet how many times have you been required to stay up late or pull an all-nighter to complete a vital assignment, tender, or paper?

Not many businesses and organisations would tolerate staff

turning up to work intoxicated. It's a pretty quick route to losing your job. Yet tiredness is apparently acceptable despite it having the same disastrous effect on thinking, concentration, memory, and performance.

The blue light emitted by your screen confuses your pineal gland, a tiny organ located deep in your brain that recognises when the day is finished. Normally, as daylight fades, your brain starts to prepare itself to quieten down ready for sleep. Your choice to stay up late to watch a movie or work on your laptop persuades your brain that it is still daytime. Your neurons keep firing at a higher rate, which helps you to keep going, even though you may cognitively be very tired. Yet when it is finally time to snuggle down under the doona, your brain isn't ready to switch off.

Insufficient or poor-quality sleep disrupts your ability to take in new information and retain it as memory. Sleep is vital for memory consolidation, absorbing new information, verbal memory, emotional regulation, and mood. It is also vital for creative thinking and problem solving.

Have you noticed the impact of sleep deprivation on your own brain? It's not uncommon to associate tiredness with a grumpy and uncooperative mood. Snapping at your co-workers or family doesn't win you any brownie points, and that negative emotion is highly contagious. Everyone starts acting a little cranky.

Tiredness puts you at greater risk of developing a mood disorder such as anxiety and depression. In fact, it is now thought that the sleep disturbance many people experience with these forms of mental illness can actually precipitate their development, as well as exacerbate the problems associated with them.

The trouble is, as so many people are chronically sleep deprived, they have probably forgotten what it's like to have a good night's sleep.

How much sleep you need is something that is unique to you. Seven to eight hours is considered the norm, but you may be someone who can do very well on four hours or you may need ten. You know you are getting enough good-quality sleep if you wake up feeling refreshed and fully recharged.

TIPS FOR OVERCOMING SLEEP DEPRIVATION

1. Take a nap.
Some business are now starting to recognise how important sleep is for performance, and companies such as Google have installed Sleep Pods in the workplace, where tired employees can take a 20-minute, reviving nap. The impact of taking a short nap can be to boost cognitive performance by 30 to 40% for a couple of hours. They have also instigated sleep awareness programs in the workplace.

2. Change your work schedule.
Do you have to work so late at night? Can you change your roster or how it is set up? Does your workplace facilitate more flexible working hours to enable you to get adequate breaks between shifts?

3. Set a time limit for how late you work at night.
If your bedtime is 10.30, then ideally all work should be finished by between 7.30 and 8.30 pm. In 2011 Volkswagen introduced a policy whereby their server is switched off between 7 pm and 7 am to ensure staff weren't taking their work home with them.

4. Change the work culture from "more is good" to "less can be better".

Studies have revealed how productivity actually goes up when the total number of projects being dealt with is reduced. Spreading ourselves too thin contributes to fatigue and overwork. Certain organisations will have particularly busy times, such as the end of the financial year. Reducing the cultural expectation of overwork is the first step to promoting a culture in which employee brain health and function takes priority.

5. Establish good sleep hygiene.

By this I mean establish a routine that promotes the likelihood of your getting a good night's sleep by setting up a wind-down routine to prepare your brain for sleep, and avoiding anti-sleep items such as caffeine, alcohol, and late-night action movies during this period.

6. Turn off that blue light.

The answer here is to work out a way for you to shut down those screens *two to three hours* before you want to go to sleep.

FOSTERING A NAP-FRIENDLY WORKPLACE

Not all business organisations are going to be convinced by your suggestion that everyone take a brief nap during the day to boost creativity, focus and energy. Sleep deprivation is not only bad for people's brains and health, it's bad for business. So this is a good time to start exploring with your colleagues how naps could be integrated into your workplace with the expected benefits of having more brains fully charged and fully functional for longer.

For more information about the role of lifestyle choice to enhance your brain's fitness, my book *Brain Fit* covers all the key essentials necessary for every brain to become optimised to function at its best.

What are some strategies that you can use to ensure you keep your brain and those of others safe in your workplace?

1. **Regulate your workload.**

Recognise the delicate power struggle going on constantly between the slower frontal lobes, our executive thinking; and the limbic system, our fast, feisty emotional self. Check in regularly by just taking a moment to pause and ask:

- Am I feeling okay about my workload?
- Am I making uncharacteristic mistakes or forgetting things I wouldn't normally forget?
- Am I doing everything in a rush and cutting corners I wouldn't normally cut?

2. **Recognise the limitation to your working memory capacity.**

Be aware that your working memory has limited working space and there is often a bottleneck of information waiting to be handled and passed over to long-term storage. Can you structure your work into smaller chunks to help your brain run more efficiently?

3. **Notice your stress alarm.**

Recognise when your red warning light for too much stress is flashing early enough, and have the strategies in place to quickly restore balance. This could include:

(a) **Allocate time just for you** every day. Schedule in ten minutes of down time in which to stop and relax. Allocate this time to listen to music you like, to practise a short meditation, to take a walk in the fresh air, or just to sit in the office alone with the door shut and *no* interruptions.

(b) **Take regular holidays**, real holidays. What is the point of taking leave if you spend it still attached to the umbilical cord of your laptop and mobile phone? Turn them off. If you think you are that indispensable to your workplace, who are you kidding and who is kidding you?

(c) **Do some physical exercise**. Regularly. Thirty minutes of physical exercise helps you to burn off nervous tension and reduces the level of stress hormones currently bathing your brain.

(d) **Check in to see what facilities** your workplace provides to help manage stress. Many workplaces now provide access to gyms, yoga, or meditation classes.

(e) **Get help as appropriate**. Talk to a friend, colleague, or family member with whom you feel safe discussing your issues. Simply sharing what is worrying you can take a huge weight off your mind, and it helps your brain to work through them and find solutions.

CHAPTER 2

DO WE STILL NEED MEMORY NOW WE HAVE GOOGLE?

Today we have a level of accessibility to information via the World Wide Web (the web) that we would never previously have thought possible. Just a few keystrokes and we can access everything we need in a matter of seconds.

A generation or two back, students in school were expected to learn material by rote. We had to learn poems and stories by heart and be able to recite them in class when called upon. Long-term memory has been crucial in our evolution, allowing us to pass on our acquired knowledge from generation to generation. The written word, which has been available to us for only around 5000 years, revolutionised how we communicated and shared information.

How we use the Internet today suggests the need to once again re-evaluate how we communicate and share information. Do we still even need to learn information? Our education system continues to assess students on their ability to regurgitate information they have formatted in their memory, as a measure of academic success. However, success in life today depends mainly on how we manipulate and use information available to us, rather than on our capacity to remember it.

Our social brain has provided us with the skills to share knowledge and information. This valuable skill means we don't have to start from scratch every time we need to solve a problem or work out how to do something.

If you have ever taken part in a team quiz game, you will know that the best team to be part of is one where each individual has access to unique knowledge relating to their work or life interests. I can be helpful on the medical questions but am absolutely useless when it comes to knowing who won a particular football match, let alone who the players were. So it can be really useful to have someone who follows sport, or who is a music buff — and of course someone with a good grounding in general knowledge.

Sharing information is called transactive memory. The benefit, of course, is that not everyone needs to know everything (this is neither desirable nor practical). This frees up more space in our prefrontal cortices to remember what is pertinent to our own requirements.

Beyond quiz games, the one place we go to consistently to access information today is the web. Yet how well do we retain the information we obtain from this source? This was a question Columbia University psychologist Betsy Sparrow[14] and her team of researchers set out to answer. She found that in addition to our expectation of being able to find the information we seek online, was the fact that unless we know or think we might need to remember it in the future, we don't.

As Roddy Roediger, a psychologist from Washington University, said as part of a commentary on the Sparrow research paper, "Why remember something if I know I can look it up again?" What makes the difference in our online information acquisition is whether we have been told that we need to remember the information.

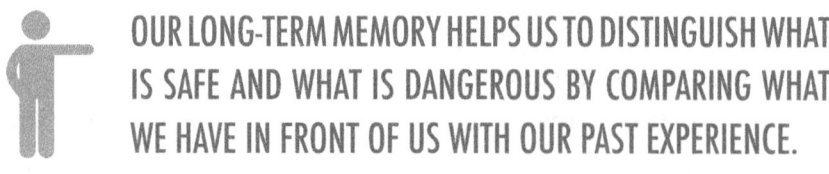

OUR LONG-TERM MEMORY HELPS US TO DISTINGUISH WHAT IS SAFE AND WHAT IS DANGEROUS BY COMPARING WHAT WE HAVE IN FRONT OF US WITH OUR PAST EXPERIENCE.

WHY LONG-TERM MEMORIES ARE LIKE CATCHING FISH

We've all heard stories about "the one that got away", and of course the fish gets bigger with every telling. Our ability to catch those slippery thoughts and ideas and translate them into long-term storage data is what counts.

Our long-term memory helps us to distinguish what is safe and what is dangerous by comparing what we have in front of us with our past experience. It helps us determine whether a food is safe to eat, or whether going into business with that other person is something we should contemplate doing.

Our long-term memory storage system is highly complex and extremely fragile. Forming memory integrates a number of processes starting with attention, and includes determining the degree of value, immediacy of need, or relevance for consideration for filing for long-term access. Then, of course, there are all those other factors that influence our ability to complete this activity, including how much sleep we are getting, our health, our distractibility, our mood, our stress levels, and our environment, to mention just a few!

If we are continually interrupted or distracted, the chance of these fragile memories being retained is drastically reduced. It's a bit like turtle hatchlings. Hundreds may hatch from the nest but with persistent attacks by hungry seagulls and other predators, fighting against ocean currents, and the challenge of finding enough food, little wonder that only one in a thousand will survive into adulthood.

Today, with so many distractions vying for our attention, our ability to manage our attention is constantly being tested. As a consequence, many of us have developed poor thinking habits through which we set ourselves up to remember less.

One area of the brain that is vital for memory formation is the hippocampus. This is the area in the temporal lobe where memories are sifted and sorted. Like the rest of the brain it is highly plastic, which means the more it is used, the greater the number of synaptic connections made between brain cells, which actually increases its volume.

Born in the UK, I spent some time living and working in London. One thing I always knew I could count on was that any Black Cab taxi driver would know exactly how to get to my required destination, and the quickest route to take. London cabbies traditionally have had to learn 'The Knowledge', comprising over twenty-five thousand streets and all the various permutations of how to get from A to B in the shortest time. It takes an average of two years for London cabbies to imprint these spatial maps in their brains sufficiently well to pass the very stringent tests required to gain a licence to drive one of the famous Black Cabs.

Back in 2000, some fascinating research[15] was done examining the brains of taxi drivers to look at what effect acquiring this knowledge had on their brains. It was found that the posterior part of their hippocampus, the area of the brain associated with spatial navigation, grew bigger. Neuroplasticity in action! Moreover, the longer the cabbie had spent acquiring the knowledge, the greater the increase in volume of this area of their brain.

The key to learning a new skill or embedding a new habit is repetition. The more a new neural pathway is restimulated, the stronger and more robust it becomes, so eventually it requires very little stimulus to fire it up. This is the principle of Hebb's Law [16]:

Cognitive reserve is the term used in brain fitness, where stimulating your brain's natural plasticity through enhancing the formation of new synaptic connections and circuits to produce a stronger, more resilient brain, is of particular value in safeguarding our brain against future cognitive decline. Greater neuroplasticity doesn't occur just through practising new skills, it can occur even as a result of our imagination.

Back in 1995, neuroscientist Professor Alvaro Pascual-Leone[17] undertook a couple of experiments examining how the brain changes when learning to play music. In the first experiment he taught a group of subjects a simple one-handed five-finger exercise on the piano. The subjects had to practise for two hours a day for five days, playing as fluently as they could in time to a metronome set at 60 beats a minute. What he found on TMS mapping (a technique for examining neuronal function in certain areas of the brain) was that five days was long enough to show a physiological change in the motor cortex, in that more neurons became involved in performing the new function.

He then repeated the experiment, but this second group simply imagined doing the practice. The result? Those who had imagined themselves undertaking the practice showed almost the same increase in neuronal activity as those who had actually practised.

The lesson here is that envisioning and mentally rehearsing a new skill or technique, such as improving your tennis serve or golf swing, will translate into a physiological response in your brain's neural architecture.

Strengthening neural pathways will always depend on the initial practice period. If you look at this from an evolutionary point of view, the art of writing, using words to describe experiences or share information, is a relatively recent phenomenon, evolving from early cave art to hieroglyphics to the alphabets we know today. We learned to write using a stylus, a quill fashioned from a feather, and then a pen. Today we use keypads and touch screens, which has revolutionised the way and the speed in which we communicate with one another. As we have adapted to our new technology our speed and effort required to use these tools changes and improves. Watch any teenager texting their friends and marvel at the speed of their fingers nimbly crafting messages in the blink of an eye. Likewise avid video-gamers manipulating their consoles with speed and agility far unlike my own slow and lumbering fat-fingered efforts.

One thing that differentiates the modern brain from that of our forbears, is firstly our ability to adapt and learn these new skills more quickly, and secondly our capacity to practise these new skills much faster than in any previous generations.

WHY MEMORY IS FLUKEY

David and Celia were at a dinner party when David started to tell the story of a recent event that he and Celia had both attended. As David recounted his shaggy dog tale, Celia grew increasingly uncomfortable until at last she blurted out, "But David, that's not how it was at all! We were in Dunsborough, not Augusta, and we were with Nigel and Alice, not Pete and Sue."

In the workplace, knowing how to recall a salient piece of information at the appropriate time is vital. Yet just how accurate are your memories? Every time you recall a particular piece of information, accessing the relevant components of that memory requires your brain to integrate those separate neural circuits and put them back together to create a whole.

The trouble is, each time our brain goes through this process the memory becomes more "flexible" or modifiable. Our most recent memories are most prone to this, and this means our memories are

LOSS OF HIPPOCAMPAL VOLUME DUE TO SEVERE STRESS IN MIDLIFE

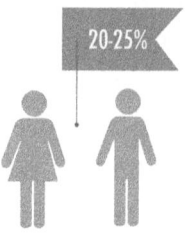

highly suggestible to being changed. You might remember that the colour of a jacket worn by a friend to a party was red, but the first time you recall it differently, or *someone else* recalls it differently, prompts your memory to change the remembered facts. The jacket may now be remembered as being blue.

Which is why you sometimes hear disagreements between people who were at the same event and have a completely different recall of who said what to whom, who wore what, and so on.

In our judicial system our reliance on witnesses recalling events is highly questionable because our memories are so flukey, even though we believe them to be reliable.

The question then becomes who, if anyone, is right?

It has been said that the more strongly an emotion is attached to a memory, the less likely it is subject to be altered in this way. Yet research has shown that even the strongest emotional recollections — for example, those of 9/11 witnesses to the collapse of the Twin Towers — do not make our memories of these events immune to this effect.

Another major influence on our memory and retention is stress. Studies of the brains of severely stressed 40- to 50-year-olds revealed a loss in hippocampal volume of between 20 and 25%.[18] Our hippocampus, which is vital for long-term memory, is extremely sensitive to environmental influences, so watch that stress dial!

Chronic severe depression[19] is known to have a similar effect on hippocampal function and volume. This means if you are severely depressed you will have a much harder job remembering things. This is also true, of course, for those unfortunate enough to develop Alzheimer's disease,[20] for whom the earliest loss of brain function involves the hippocampus.

Eventually though, our long-term memories do become more fixed. That's why sometimes our most reliable memories can be the oldest ones. One of my earliest memories is as a young girl aged about three standing on a concrete ramp leading down to the beach at Tenby in Wales, although how much this is an actual memory of the event or is influenced by the photograph that was taken at the time, I can't actually be sure!

WHY REMEMBERING TAKES AGES

For many businesses and organisations, innovation and new ideas need to be shared and implemented quickly, but in an environment where little time is available and budgets are tight, traditional methods of training are increasingly recognised as inadequate and ineffective.

In our work we need to take in new information, determine its relevance or value, and decide whether to keep it, where to keep it now, how to apply it, and where to store it for future reference. In other words, we need to know how to filter out what we need and then make sure the learning sticks.

Susan had been chosen to attend a three-day conference which outlined a new system that her bosses wanted implemented in their organisation. Following the conference, she was asked to debrief her team on the key points and outline how the new system could best be integrated into the business.

Susan had thoroughly enjoyed the event. She was very impressed by what she heard, and thought the new system would be very useful to the organisation. The three days had been jam-packed, with a full program of speakers, workshops, and breakout sessions. In addition, Susan had attended the extra breakfast sessions, and came away with a stack of notes and handouts (and a headache). However, when it came to recalling the salient information, Susan found herself struggling to articulate what she had learned, and what would be useful to her company.

Pushing too much information over extended days in a short period of time has been the typical conference format for many years. The problem is it's a terrible way for brains to absorb new ideas and content.

In 2010 Davachi, Kiefer and Rock[21] wrote a paper outlining a model that draws together current thinking about the most effective way to maximise learning. This model is called AGES, which stands for:

- **Attention** — paying attention to the subject matter being learned

- **Generation** — personalising the information so that it has meaning for the individual

- **Emotion** — enhancing the attention being spent on the task, and in addition activating the amygdala, which helps to increase the effectiveness of encoding memory

- **Spacing** — distributing the learning over time, leading to better long-term memory and higher retrieval rates. Spacing can appear to make the learning harder, but it is the additional effort required of the brain to retrieve the information that makes the memories stick better.

If your work or organisation requires you to attend training programs, adopting brain-friendly learning practices will greatly elevate the effectiveness or return on investment of the training. Considering the amount of time, effort and cost it takes to make training available, it would seem a no-brainer to ensure that all attendees are guaranteed to learn what is required in such a way as to be able to implement it immediately in their work place.

Things to consider include:

- **The format of engagement** with the new material — maybe rethinking how a training day is set up and how material is presented and shared.

- **Ensuring that even the shortest attention spans** can continue to be refocused on the material being presented.

- **Chunking down the learning** into a series of shorter modules of one to two hours or a "lunch n' learn".

- **Improving retention of knowledge** — by creating a richer network of associations around the material, enhancing insight into the relevance of the new learning, and testing what has been remembered.

- **Raising positive emotion** during the learning experience. If you think back to school, which were the teachers who inspired you the most? Arousing our emotional amygdala also stimulates the hippocampus, which helps us to retain new information. Our Goldilocks brain will always stipulate the need for balance though, as too much emotion, whether positive or negative, will shut the hippocampus down.

Spacing the information is what counts. Growing new dendrites — that is, forming new synaptic connections between our neurons — takes time. It is a biological process. Spacing gives the brain time to forget. Once you have learned something new, there is a natural decline in what you store as memory. Making your brain work harder to remember this information using revision and testing is what matters. So ideally, we need to revise the salient points within 24 hours, and then again the following week by asking our brains to jot down the important facts that we can remember.

Remembering what matters starts with the headlines. Our brain finds it quite easy to then fill in the rest of the story with the other details. This filtering, by starting with the big items, is important so the brain doesn't become overloaded with trivia while missing the important concepts.

Shortly after my husband and I first moved to Perth, we were introduced to a new activity — prawning. The idea was you went down to the Swan River at dusk with a couple of prawn nets, a bucket, and a head torch. Wading through the water in the dark, you could feel the silty mud between your toes and gradually feel the net getting heavier, hopefully with lots of prawns for supper.

Then you had the fun part of sorting through your catch and taking home your prize. The vital component of a successful prawning outing was the net. If the holes were too small you caught everything, including half the river's weed. Too big, and those prawns would wriggle their way to freedom in a jiffy. In the same way, how your brain retains memories relies on having the right-size net to consistently capture those memories you do want while discarding what you don't need.

We also now know that matching the learning environment to *where* you recall the information matters for how well you remember it. Experiments[22] conducted back in the 1970s revealed the importance of context for memory retention in a group of subjects who were asked to learn a series of 80 different words, and then asked to recall them either:

- in the same room where they originally learned them
- in a different room
- in a different room while being asked to visualise the place they had learned the words.

The results showed that matching the learning and retrieval environment made the difference. Follow-up experiments[23] took this one step further, with the original learning taking place either on dry land or underwater, and recall being required either in the same environment or in the other environment. Recall was consistently 50% higher when the learning and recall took place in the same context even when this was under water.

That doesn't necessarily imply that you can only learn effectively by being in the same place all the time. Wesley Verhoeve[24] believes changing our learning environment is good for creativity. In his view, choosing to work occasionally from a coffee shop rather than your office, and by breaking your general routine jolts the brain out of complacency by exposing your mind to a new environment. Obviously, this may work better for some people than for others, and also depends on how your own work environment is set up. There may not always be the opportunity for this kind of variation. I certainly enjoy a change periodically, and use the more relaxed venue of a café to think and to connect with other brains. Whether I really get more creative work done there is debatable, though I certainly drink more coffee!

One other technique to enhance learning follows on from the piano playing experiments using visual imagery. This is where you revise using your own mental images of the diagrams and data remembered. Using visual imagery has also been used in psychological goal setting for a long time.[25] Michael Jordan is well known for espousing the value of imagining yourself as already having achieved the outcome you desire. What is fascinating is the physiological change revealed on brain scans when people engage in this technique. That's why going over information when studying is crucial to helping the brain retain it as memory and make it more accessible for recall.

> **In summary, the three essentials to better learning are:**
> - **the *timing* of the repetition**
> - **the *location* of the repetition**
> - **the *insights* generated to deepen the learning.**

BRINGING THE CLASS TO ATTENTION

Using our frontal lobes to pay attention is a complex process. Psychologist Michael Posner[26], from the University of Oregon, is a world expert on attention whose studies have revealed that paying attention requires three separate neural functions.

1. **Be alert.** Being awake is always a good start to paying attention. Then, of course, we have to maintain that alert state and not allow our attention to drift off, as it is so prone to do.

2. **Be orientated.** No, this does not relate to an orienteering course, but it does suggest that you need to judge which sensory focus is most appropriate for the task at hand. If you are listening to a conversation, then you are orienting your focus to hearing. If you are watching a presentation, you are orienting your focus to include vision and hearing.

3. **Engage your executive attention.** This means using your frontal lobes and an area of your brain called the *cingulate gyrus* to regulate other neural networks relating to your emotions and other sensory input. This is what matters to achieve higher mental performance.

In other words, paying attention requires you to be awake, focused on what is relevant to you right now, and able to divert sufficient energy and effort into the process for long enough to achieve your goal.

When you are not paying attention the brain is often described as a noisy, chaotic place. Choosing to focus can be compared to the moment when the conductor of a symphony orchestra, with a couple of taps of his baton on the music stand, brings all the different instruments, hitherto making a cacophony of noise as they are being tuned, into perfect synchronised harmony as they start to produce beautiful music.

ATTENTION CHANGES OUR BRAIN

Paying attention literally changes our brain, because the process of focus prompts our brain to form multiple new connections or synapses. The more connections we form, the stronger and more resilient our brain becomes. We are truly lifelong learners.

This is the beauty of having a plastic brain, a brain that is dynamic and with the capacity to rewire itself constantly, 24/7, in response to the stimuli it receives. This takes place all the time; it's natural and normal and you don't have to do anything to make it happen. The response to a new stimulus is for our neurons to form new synaptic connections. Repetition of the same stimulus will further develop and strengthen these new neural circuits. This is how we learn new information, lay down memory, and develop new skills and behaviours.

How long is your attention? This is a bit like asking how long is a piece of string. Previous studies determined the average attention span as being around 10 to 12 minutes up until around ten years ago, but it has been suggested that this has since been eroded by up to 40% *simply as a consequence* of the way in which we live our lives today.

So what do we need to do to help stop ourselves ending up with the attention span of a goldfish (currently thought to be about three minutes)? We can start by finding novelty in what we pay attention to. Novelty stimulates our brain. In a classroom, for example, a teacher might ask a question, show a picture, or move to a different part of the room. Our brain wants to be entertained, so somehow we need to find a new or alternative source of entertainment every few minutes to help the brain stay focused.

WHAT DO WE NEED TO DO TO HELP STOP OURSELVES ENDING UP WITH THE ATTENTION SPAN OF A GOLDFISH?

That's why brain training requires us to learn something new that we haven't encountered before. You may have studied the saxophone years ago. Dusting off the instrument that has been sitting under the hall stairs for 30 years is a good way to strengthen existing neural circuits that may have got a bit rusty. An even more effective way to train your brain would be to take up a different instrument, or to learn a new language, or a new sport.

Keep the information relevant to what interests you. If you are learning about nuclear physics but your passion is music, it's going to be a lot harder for you to maintain attention.

Though sometimes we *have to* pay attention to what we don't find interesting. What then?

The temptation is to switch off or start doing something else, but there are techniques you can apply other than pinching yourself to stay awake. Taking notes, asking questions, doodling, chewing gum, and looking for something, anything, that would enable you to usefully apply the information in your life are all ways you can use distractions in a positive way to help in this situation.

INCREASING ATTENTION DENSITY

Jeffrey Schwartz[27], author of *You Are Not Your Brain*, defines attention density as the amount of attention we pay to any one particular mental experience over a period of time. The greater your concentration or focus, the higher your attention density. Focusing your attention on a particular thought or action or mental image stimulates your brain's plasticity, strengthening those neural pathways associated with this experience that lead ultimately to a physiological change within the brain.

That's how we know that focus reshapes our brain. We all have a unique neural architecture, and how we use our brain helps to maintain its uniqueness. If you are a musician, for example, your focus will be on those things that are relevant to your world — playing, remembering or writing music. The focus of a scientist will be on research and studies relating to his or her work.

Scientists and musicians have their own sets of neural connections that dictate how they perceive the world. In business too, what we focus on, using a different set of connections, determines the way we think. Knowing this provides you with the tools you need to move from mere knowledge acquisition to implementing a new way of thinking.

As previously discussed, attending a workshop or presentation can provide you with a whole raft of new ideas, concepts and strategies that could be really helpful to you if implemented. The problem that is experienced time and time again with this type of training, is that on its own, it is ineffective.

Have you ever had that experience where you walked out of a workshop and went back to the office or back home and shared your thoughts about how great it was, how good the presenter was, how useful the information was — and yet you find yourself struggling to come up with any of the key points discussed and covered?

Perhaps that's why businesses often see such little return on investment from the training programs their staff attend. It's not that they weren't listening; it's that the brain needs more than one application of information, and more than one type of information processing, to really grasp and embed a new thought pattern.

A study at Baruch College, New York, in 1997 by Olivero, Bane and Kopelman[28] found that training programs alone led to an increase in productivity of 28%. Supplementing them with follow-up coaching, however, led to an 88% increase in productivity.

> **Long-term change requires ongoing attention, in the same way you would revise for an exam. Effective learning therefore may involve four steps:**
> 1. **Attending the lecture/training session**
> 2. **Paying attention to the lecturer/trainer**
> 3. **Taking notes of the salient points (on paper or a laptop or tablet)**
> 4. **Revising the information.**

The crucial step is the revision, which needs to be done repeatedly over time to really embed the new information into your brain's existing architecture.

Kristen Hansen[29], from Enhansen Performance, suggests you need to pay attention to the information or goal three times a day initially to really embed it into your brain. Secondhand information is never retained quite as well, which is why online lectures are never as good as face-to-face presentations, and neither are someone else's notes.

Ways to increase your attention density can include:

- **Arrive early** or in good time before a presentation or meeting to get your brain into "ready" mode with *conscious* attention.

- **Take brain breaks.** If you are at a full-day conference or workshop, ensure you take regular brain breaks of 10–15 minutes to reflect on and consider what you have been learning.

- **Chunk down** the salient points into bite-sized pieces your brain can handle. Remember, the average brain can only hold around 7 pieces of information in its working memory at any one time. The more complex the items, the fewer our brain can retain.

- **Practise and rehearse** the new ideas and thoughts that induce a positive response in your brain. Focusing on *what can be done* induces a "towards" response in the brain that enhances the development of that thinking pattern.

- **Allow sufficient time for rehearsal** so you are thinking at a deeper level. This also engages your subconscious thinking, which can begin contributing to automating the new skill or habit.

- **Avoid focusing on what doesn't work**, and the associated problems and obstacles, because focusing on the negative enhances those negative neural pathways, which is not the desired outcome! The brain is constantly looking for opportunities to create new pathways and prune back those no longer considered necessary. Focusing on the positive affords the opportunity for the negatives to be pruned back.

- **Focus on your strengths** as this is what leads to professional growth and development. The SWOT method of recognising your weak spots and working on them is less likely to produce the required change, because by focusing on the negatives you strengthen the "away" response in your brain.

- **Utilise** *attentional retraining* using online computerised cognitive training. This was originally introduced for cognitive rehabilitation following brain injury. More recently, working memory training has become popular as a means to enhance mental flexibility and agility, as both are very useful qualities in today's increasingly complex world.

STRENGTHENING YOUR ATTENTIONAL MUSCLE

The capacity to re-engage our brain and enhance our attention skills is crucial in today's learning and work environments. Fortunately, learning to enhance our ability to pay attention is quite simple: it is really a case of recognising you could do better and then putting your strategy into practice.

You can:

1. **Focus on reading** an article or passage of a book for a predetermined time, say 20 minutes, and then recalling the key features or message.

2. **Play games such as chess or bridge.**

3. **Play action video games.** While some people hate action video games because of their tendency to include violence and their potentially addictive nature, these types of games have been shown to offer a number of cognitive benefits, including enhancing focus and reducing the amount of brain energy spent on managing distractions. They are also really good for enhancing visual spatial skills. A very interesting study[30] published in 2013 revealed that surgeons who play action video games in their leisure time have superior technical and attention skills when undertaking laparoscopic procedures on their patients.

4. **Cut the caffeine and other stimulants,** which fire up your brain cells to work faster but don't improve performance and, overall, add to

fatigue levels. Caffeine competes with a natural brain chemical called adenosine. During the day your adenosine levels gradually rise, allowing the brain to recognise it is time to start slowing down your mental activity and preparing for sleep. If the adenosine receptors are blocked by caffeine, they keep firing at a higher rate, which is useful in the short term if you have to keep working a little longer. Eventually, you'll reach cognitive exhaustion, which is often the time you decide you need another coffee!

5. Get enough sleep. The first thing that starts to fail when we are a bit tired is our ability to think, to learn new information, and to concentrate. Sleep is essential for memory consolidation and to get the real "gist" of what we have learned. It's also critical for mood and emotional regulation. If you have ever lived with sleep-deprived and cranky toddlers (or grown-ups) you will know what this is like.

6. Eat something. Brain cells chew up more energy than many other cells in your body. It takes a lot of energy to think, and especially to pay focused attention. Your brain may comprise only 2% of your body weight, but it consumes around 25% of all the energy you take in everyday. Ideally, take in food every few hours to keep your blood sugar levels steady. If you are mentally tired and running low on willpower, one glass of lemonade (ideally fresh) may make all the difference.

7. Do some exercise. Using your other muscles helps your mental muscle to work more effectively. Choose one form of aerobic activity that you can spend 30–60 minutes doing every day to get your attention really sharpened up. Exercise boosts the release of brain chemicals, including brain-derived neurotrophic factor (BDNF for short). This is vital for neuron maintenance, synaptic strengthening, and stimulating neurogenesis — the birth, maturation, and integration of new brain cells or neurons.

8. Relax. Paradoxically, your ability to relax and tune out enhances your brain's ability to be focused when required. Your brain was designed to stay focused for short periods of time only. Tuning out enables greater focus when next required, and stimulates greater innovative and creative thinking. It's also when you will enjoy a higher level of insight.

9. Engage in social activities. Social interactions stimulate the brain. You benefit from shared information and ideas, which allows your plastic brain to create new neural pathways, new neural maps and, again, promote better problem solving, insight, judgement, and creativity.

10. Be more mindful. An eight-week mindfulness program can enhance focus and awareness, stabilise mood, and clarify thinking. Along with exercise, becoming more mindful is one of the most powerful tools available to us to rebuild focus.

11. Reward your focus. The brain likes to move us towards something that makes us feel good. Rewarding your improved attention skills can work as a powerful motivator to help you keep up your practice.

12. Manage all of your interruptions. This is not so hard once you have identified the culprits and learned how best to manage them, which is what we will cover in the next chapter.

CHAPTER 3

NOT DESIGNED FOR LONG-TERM FOCUS

"I'll be back around four, honey." Gary was on his way to catch up with some mates who shared a common passion in all things to do with aircraft and flying. He zoomed out the back door towards the car as his wife called out, "Don't forget we're due at the restaurant at seven!" It was their wedding anniversary and plans were in place for a big family dinner.

Gary loved his little plane and once down at the hangar would hunker down, tinkering with the aircraft engine, and chat with his aircraft buddies. He was so absorbed in his intricate rewiring project, which was taking a bit longer than he had hoped, that he didn't notice the lengthening shadows outside or even the onset of darkness. It was only when his growling stomach made him realise he hadn't stopped for lunch, that he checked his mobile phone to find it was already well past 7 and there were a string of missed text messages and voicemails waiting for him.

Yes, Gary was in the doghouse that night and for a few nights thereafter!

Have you ever been with someone who was so focused on what they were doing that they were completely oblivious to everything else around them? Psychologist Mihaly Csikszentmihalyi[31], in his book *Flow*, explores what contributes to a life worth living; in particular those activities that we find provide the greatest pleasure and lasting satisfaction. When we are *in flow* we are totally absorbed, time becomes irrelevant, and we find everything seems to come together easily and naturally. A great place to find yourself in, yet there are times when being single-minded about what we give our attention to can cause us to miss out big time elsewhere.

Naturally, we think that because we are walking around with our eyes open we are taking in everything around us, or at least all that's relevant to our needs and safety. Well, not quite. Yes, we do keep our eyes open, but the amount of information our brain actually uses is a fraction of what is available. Otherwise, our brain would be overloaded with too much information, much of it irrelevant to us. Our brain has to filter what is appropriate to us.

When we are looking at something in a focused way, sometimes the brain becomes essentially "blind" for a short period of time. No, it's not just because you blink, although the phenomenon is called *attentional blink*. The human brain is exceedingly good at noticing error or change. Though once your brain has registered this, it takes up to half a second for your brain to recalibrate, meaning that if another change is flashed up before you in that time frame, you simply won't see it.

The other thing about focusing hard is that we don't always see what else is going on around us. If you are watching a football game and following the person in control of the ball at the time, you may not see another adjacent player deliberately tripping up his opponent.

Don't believe me? Well, you may also be familiar with the Invisible

Gorilla Experiment by Christopher Chabris and Daniel Simons[32], in which the subjects were asked to focus their attention on certain activity in a basketball game. In their desire to focus really closely, however, they failed to notice something else in the video that was glaringly out of place. When the video was replayed, the participants were astounded they had missed something so obvious. I have replayed this video dozens of times and I can still fool my brain into not seeing it! The strange thing is, even if you know the twist to this experiment, you will still be no better at picking up an unexpected event elsewhere when focusing on other tasks. It's just how our brain works.

Practising broadening your awareness of your environment beyond your immediate point of focus can help, but it does take practice.

The point is that in our constant state of busyness, we can miss so much by failing to see other potential opportunities outside our own point of focus or context.

In another famous experiment,[33] a busker played violin on a suburban metro platform in Washington DC during the morning rush hour. Over one thousand commuters swept by but only seven people stopped to listen, and in over 45 minutes he earned a measly few dollars for his efforts. Which was a shame considering he was Joshua Bell, one of the world's foremost violinists, playing Bach on a 300-year-old Stradivarius violin.

The point is that in our constant state of busyness, we can miss so much by failing to see other potential opportunities outside our own point of focus or context.

 ## YOUR BEST IDEAS SURFACE WHEN YOU ARE NOT FOCUSED, SUCH AS WHEN YOU ARE IN THE SHOWER OR WALKING ALONG A BEACH.

Have you ever had a golden opportunity sitting right under your nose that you simply failed to notice? Being over focused not only causes rapid mental fatigue, but also denies your brain the ability to create insight. Those wonderful "aha" moments come along, not when we are most focused, but paradoxically when we are defocused, when our brain can access those quieter thoughts to form new patterns of thinking.

That's why you have your best ideas in the shower, while walking the dogs along the beach, or even while talking to a friend about something else.

How does your workplace measure up in encouraging innovation and creativity? Is it merely paying lip service to the idea of valuing innovative ideas but not really wanting them to be presented? Is that because of a culture of "that's the way it has always been done around here"?

How can you set up the right conditions for more insightful thinking in your place of work? Brainstorming is often used as a way to brain dump new ideas yet this process, unless handled well, can actually stifle creative thinking. Our intense focus and involvement with ideas emanating from other people's brains may blinker us to considering our own alternative perspectives, which might be even better than the ones being proposed by others! Yes, brainstorming can work, but sometimes we come up with our best ideas working quietly on our own.

Good brainstorming sessions permit all voices to be heard equally. This is no place for judgement but a melting pot for all ideas, each to be considered on its own merit. These can then be whittled down to find the one really good idea to be taken away and implemented.

OUR SHRINKING ATTENTION SPAN

One of the main concerns relating to our attention span is how fast it is shrinking. The original studies of university students reading a chapter of *War and Peace* (I'm sure you have read it too, right?) showed that the average attention span (at least for a university student) was consistently around 12 minutes. Yet this span has now been reported to have dropped, in some instances, to as little as five to eight minutes. Why?

It's basically because the way we use our brain has changed. For example, when playing a video game you need your brain to be highly focused and very fast. The aim of action video games is to score points as fast as possible in order to win the game and, more importantly, to increase your standing on the score board against others playing the same game. Setting aside for a moment the fact that the most successful action video games appear to be centred on killing people, every time you score a point, "Ping", your brain experiences a reward in the form of a little squirt of dopamine, your feel-good neurotransmitter. The more "Pings", the more dopamine, and just like the other rewards your brain experiences with other pleasurable experiences, such as having sex or consuming drugs, your brain wants more please, and now!

It's the same when sending a text message or email. How delicious for your brain to experience that almost instant reward of a response from the person you just messaged. You can feel that dopamine surging now.

Your brain is a simple creature really. It just wants to keep you safe and enjoying having fun, eating, and having sex. Being part of the reward mechanism, the dopamine release sets up your brain to seek that same impulse again, and soon. We communicate with others because it could lead to an opportunity for reward through something social. "Let's catch up for coffee, or a sexual liaison, your place or mine? Or a business meeting for 10 am today to discuss..."

Our tempering addiction becomes harder to resist so we start to seek out responses and more "Pings". You may play more video games for longer. You start to check in on your social media sites more often. You check your phone for updates and messages more frequently. The result? You spend proportionately more time on these reward-seeking activities than on other, less rewarding stuff that's waiting to be done.

Now there's nothing wrong with reward. It's about knowing when your brain has enough to keep you moving forward purposefully in all areas of your life. It is estimated that our attention span has diminished on average by 40% since 2000, while in the US the incidence of ADHD being reported has risen by 66%.

ESTIMATES SINCE 2000

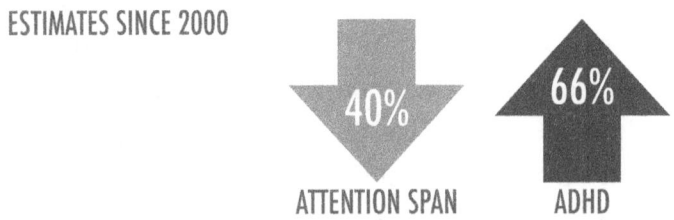

ATTENTION SPAN   ADHD

It was back in 2005 that psychiatrist Ed Hallowell[34] drew our attention to the fact that one of the consequences of our fast-paced, interconnected world is that our brains are struggling to keep up. There is now a new psychological disorder reflecting this man-made dysfunction called Attention Deficit Trait.

Happily, because the disorder is entirely of our own making and purely the consequence of how we choose to live, it is eminently treatable. The symptoms he describes for a person exhibiting ADT are remarkably similar to those for the condition Attention Deficit

Disorder:
- Black and white thinking
- Disorganised thinking
- Difficulty meeting deadlines — constantly running late
- Inability to see things clearly
- A sense of dread or guilt.

If you are finding it increasingly difficult to cope with your workload, and the expectations of others and yourself to complete your work, you could be at risk of ADT.

Psychiatrist Gary Small, head of UCLA's Memory and Aging Research Centre and author of *iBrain*, says our digital technology is not only changing the way we live and communicate with the world, it is changing our brains. His concern is that as our addiction to technology increases, our cognitive skill for decision-making, judgement, and insight decreases. He describes this as techno-brain burnout.

Our brain's plasticity means the more we use certain circuits, the stronger and more easily stimulated they become. Conversely, those being used less start to be synaptically pruned back. Those identified with Internet addiction have been shown on brain scans to have 10 to 20% smaller brain areas associated with speech, memory, motor control, emotion, sensory and other information. The old adage "use it or lose it" is true.

TIPS TO HELP OVERCOME ADT

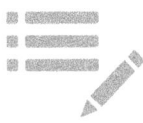

1. Categorise your work into urgent, important, necessary, and distraction categories, and then prioritise your task list. If you are putting something in the "urgent" category, check first that it really does deserve that allocation. Just because you have been asked to produce something now, it doesn't necessarily mean it should supersede the really urgent task that has been sitting quietly waiting to get done.

Avoiding distractions is good because it frees you up to spend time either doing what really matters and is relevant, or enjoying some down time. Having enough time to stop, pause and relax is as important as having enough time to complete what matters. Down time is the time to reflect and consolidate learning and memory. It is the time that allows your most creative and innovative thoughts to flow.

2. Keep the first couple of work hours for the most important and complex work you need to do that day. Your prefrontal cortex has limited capacity and is extremely energy hungry. By tackling the important stuff first and not allowing distractions to sap any precious thinking energy, you are safeguarding your brain's ability to perform at a higher level on things that need it.

That means scheduling lower priority tasks to later parts of the day.

3. Keep your list of priorities and schedule in sight during the day. This helps to remind you to stay on track. It sounds a little crazy, but it works.

4. Schedule in blocks of time for all those other important items required to maintain your brain in optimal shape. This includes time to relax, exercise, and be with family and friends. These time blocks are critical and must not be contaminated by other stuff, or work camouflaging itself as important when really it isn't.

5. Maintain the distinction between work time and personal time. Not having the time to spend with your kids, to go to a school drama production or music night or sports day even though you promised, is not on. Ever! How many times do you see parents supposedly watching their children while actually incessantly on the phone or sending emails? Three words: Don't do it! Your kids remember even if you don't.

Dr Adam Fraser, who wrote the book *The Third Space*, uses micro-transitions to help people migrate successfully from the first state of busy work, corporate thinking and business orientation, to the second state of loving husband, wife, Mum or Dad.

6. Take time out during the day for a brain break. That means taking a lunch break and several others, too. It means noticing if things are getting a little steamed up or overheated. If you are starting to feel a little frazzled, it's a sign that your brain is overloaded and needs to let off steam. You can do this by taking a walk, preferably out in the fresh air with some greenery such as trees around. Studies based on work and our environment, by Rachel and Stephen Kaplan in the 1980s, have shown that even just looking at pictures of tranquil scenes or forest is calming, so if you are completely embedded in a concrete jungle there are ways around this.

IMPROVING WORKLOAD MANAGEMENT

None of us share exactly the same workload, expectations, or capacity. Our response to how we cope on a daily basis with getting everything done will vary from person to person, day to day, and moment to moment.

However, by incorporating those strategies that are relevant to your own particular situation and needs, you can enhance your own effectiveness and productivity, and as a result, benefit from enjoying a higher level of achievement.

1. If you have too much work, ask for help. Weakness is more in the struggle and failure than in asking for some assistance. Help may not always be available but if you don't ask, you can't get. Sometimes bosses and managers have not thought through how much work may be required on a particular task or project. If you get the job done (albeit perhaps not very well), they may assume that you can cope with that workload routinely and continue to pile it on.

2. Get clarification around the task you are being asked to do. There is nothing worse than being asked to do something you don't quite understand. You feel you probably ought to know how to do it, but perhaps you haven't done it before or the format has changed. That uncertainty will lead to hesitancy and perhaps mistakes. Better to front up and check in that you have understood exactly what is being asked of you.

3. Check your mood. Yes, yours. How you present in a situation will very much depend on which mood you have chosen to display. Your behaviour reflects your internal environment. There may be some stuff happening in your life, but how you choose to respond and express your displeasure or happiness with the world is your choice and yours alone.

Putting on a smile, even if you don't feel like it, can start to improve your mood. Being in a better mood makes you more open to ideas, suggestions and alternatives, and reduces stress levels. This is where "fake it until you make it" works.

Emotion is contagious. If you are in a better mood, that will rub off on those around you. Conversely, you have probably experienced that time when you thought you were in a good mood, only to have it completely unravelled by the one person who comes into the office miserable and grouchy, and shares their misery germs.

4. Sleep. Yes, back to sleep again. We need enough sleep for proper brain function, and to manage our stress levels effectively. A tired brain is a stressed brain and that reduces cognition, learning, and memory. You will recall my earlier reference to Google and some other companies that have "sleep pods" available so tired brains can take a 20-minute nap. Cognitively refreshed, they are then able to improve performance by up to 40% for another couple of hours.

5. Establish and manage useful working relationships with others. No one is an island, or so they say. Working with other people, while sometimes stressful, is good for our social cognition. We learn how to get on better with others and learn greater empathy and trust — all great ways to cut down on stress.

Having another person to chat with or talk over what may be worrying you can often help to alleviate troublesome stress and keep your concerns in perspective.

6. Exercise your body. Just like sleep, getting enough daily exercise is an excellent way to reduce stress levels, alleviate mood, and improve sleep. Thirty minutes of physical activity, enough to elevate your pulse rate and make you a bit puffed before you start your workday, is a great way to boost your attention and cognitive performance.

WHY KEEPING A STIFF UPPER LIP DOESN'T HELP

In an era in which wrinkles and frown lines are no longer tolerated, and Botox and fillers are used to smooth out the passage of time and facial expression (don't get me started), this is one thing that is absolutely, definitely, and positively not the right thing to do. Keeping a stiff upper lip in the face of adversity, difficulty, and stress has one effect and one effect only: it makes things worse.

Coming from an English background, this can be a challenge. The brain science has revealed that emotional suppression is the worst thing we can do. I have also been trained as a medical practitioner, and doctors have been typically very good at suppressing emotion.

This is because we were taught the importance of maintaining a professional manner. Weeping with your patients wasn't seen as appropriate behaviour, although thankfully today doctors and others in the caring professions are being taught alternative and more helpful methods to deal with some of the trauma, distress, and suffering we witness on a daily basis.

Battling cultural and occupational learning habits has certainly made it harder for me to learn to respond differently, so as to retain an engaged and functional prefrontal cortex. It is something I continue to have to practise to prevent old habits from creeping back in. It matters because emotional suppression has been shown to further arouse the amygdala, so you become that simmering emotional volcano. Eventually, the Mount Helena eruption occurs and there's a lot of mess to clean up afterwards.

The other thing that happens when we suppress our emotion is that others around us sense this, and this arouses *their* amygdala and elevates *their* blood pressure. It's a double whammy. Instead of just dealing with one overly brain-stressed person, you now have two.

What can you do instead?

Finding an alternative strategy is vital, as there may be many occasions when it is important not to lose your cool and to keep your brain's brakes on. Remember also that suppression has a cognitive cost: poorer concentration and memory.

PUTTING A DIFFERENT FRAME ON THINGS

Matthew Lieberman[35], a social cognitive neuroscientist, has shown that simply expressing your feelings (preferably out loud, although you can say them silently to yourself) is the first step to regaining emotional control.

- "I feel angry!"
- "I am extremely frustrated!"
- "I am so cross!"

This is called labelling. It is simple yet extremely effective at starting to calm down your brain, and of course it only takes a second or two to do. What if someone might hear you? Perhaps it's better they hear your true feelings. It may lead to frank or open discussion about the issue, which will hopefully lead towards a resolution.

Another thing to do is to give your brain a quick bit of breathing space, again by pausing and taking one or two slow, deep breaths. That can be enough time to slow the rapidly rising spiral of emotion and stop it before it gets to the critical point.

Reappraisal and reframing is extremely effective. It isn't always easy and it takes practice. So there's no time like *now* to try it out, perhaps on a relatively minor issue that is causing you stress, to see how it works.

For example, you might be out enjoying a bit of peace and quiet in a sunny spot in a café. You've just ordered yourself a coffee, when a mum comes in with her young kids, who start rushing around the café annoying some of the other customers, shouting at each other and generally running amok.

How long before your level of irritation starts to rise? Five seconds? Five minutes? Eventually, many of us reach a point at which our time and enjoyment has been severely compromised and we feel compelled to do something about the situation, because the staff are taking no notice and you are concerned that someone will end up having a hot drink knocked over them.

The temptation would be to tell the young mum off, barking at her to keep her brats under better control. Yet what if you reappraised the situation? You don't know this woman. She could be a bad mum, or she could be someone with severe problems and a lot on her mind. If you allow the possibility that this situation may be out of the ordinary and that something may be wrong, you can ask her if everything is all right and is there something you could do to help, as the kids are being a bit noisy?

In a world where we often see on the news the macho posturing of leaders of different countries (especially those with nuclear warheads), it could be argued that this technique of reappraisal could be very usefully employed in international relations and diplomatic negotiations! It helps to keep things in perspective and allows other points of view to be considered, although having an initial level of insight is required to achieve this.

Catherine and Mark have worked together in the same company for a couple of years. They are both bright, articulate, capable employees who have been recognised as having potential for positions of leadership. Yet both have been observed sabotaging their chances of promotion through simmering office tensions that occasionally break out into an open slanging match.

What is the reason for all this tension?

Socks.

Yes, really.

Mark loves sport and plays a couple of games of footy for a local team after work each week. On his footy days he wears his footy socks to the office along with his suit and tie. This behaviour drives Catherine mad. She is incensed that he cannot see how this presents poorly for the rest of the organisation. She sees it as a lack of professionalism, and his persistence in continuing to wear them as a slight on her and the other staff. Catherine's suppressed anger and Mark's irritation with what he sees as a petty and irrelevant issue is spinning off onto other team members.

Simply asking them to reframe and look at the other's point of view allowed the light bulbs to go off. Catherine and Mark at last are able to see each other's perspective even if they don't agree.

What have you observed in your workplace? There may be no threat of nuclear war, but are there any simmering tensions? Is there a culture of suppression? Perhaps this is a good time to start up a discussion of how things could be done differently to enhance interpersonal relationships and communication.

Your attitude is always your choice and how you choose to respond to a person or situation will depend on your culture, your upbringing, and the amount of stress you can handle effectively without losing your cool. Remember, our interpersonal relationships are built on trust, understanding, and tolerance, and developing the skill of emotional regulation is the first step towards developing greater emotional intelligence.

MINDING YOUR MIND – FULLY

One of the most effective ways to reduce stress, hone attention, and produce clarity of thinking, even when under pressure, is mindfulness meditation. It is a mental discipline, by which learning to focus on something such as our breathing allows us to reconnect with being in the present moment.

We spend half our time either worrying about the future, what *might* happen, or ruminating about the past, what *did* happen. Practising being in the present allows us to quieten down our brain chatter so we regain focus, clarity, and calm.

How often do you hear people say they can no longer "switch off"? It's as if our busy, overstimulated, overtaxed brains have simply lost the capacity to find the off switch. We go to bed and wonder why our brain takes this not as a signal to relax and go to sleep, but to rev up and start to think even more about our worries and concerns, our thoughts whirling round in a maelstrom of relentless activity. This is not healthy for us, or our relationships.

Mindfulness meditation is one way to reconnect ourselves to the here and now. Jon Kabat-Zinn[36], who implemented his Mindfulness Stress Reduction Programs in 1979, says the practice has the effect of making time seem to slow down. Reconnecting with a feeling that you have time automatically frees up your mind to think more effectively.

The list of benefits of mindfulness appears to be growing almost daily as more research is published establishing the advantages mindfulness can bring to our lives. These include:

- Increased attention
- Better learning
- Better memory
- Better problem solving and decision making
- Clarity of thinking
- Improved sleep
- A greater sense of wellbeing
- Improved health
- Reduced stress
- Enhanced empathy
- Reduced bias
- Greater creativity
- Greater insight.

People who practise regular meditation have been shown to get more done. They are more efficient with their time and more productive. They also feel better about their efforts and their achievements. There's a lot to be said for implementing mindfulness practice into your daily schedule.

Sara Lazar[37] and others have shown in their research that meditation changes the brain. A physiological change can be demonstrated on a brain scan in as little as eight weeks: a thicker layer of grey matter develops as a consequence of enhanced neuroplasticity in the frontal lobes and the areas of the brain associated with learning and memory.

It's a simple means of tuning up the brain to facilitate self-change through greater self-awareness.

How can you incorporate mindfulness into your day? The beauty of mindfulness practice is that it doesn't have to be time-consuming. All you need is a quiet space where you will be uninterrupted for a short period of time. Just 10 minutes each day will start to bring benefits in a few weeks; practising for longer, say 20 or 30 minutes, is even better. How long you choose to spend will be determined by your lifestyle, your schedule, and what you find works best for you. There is no right or wrong. The main thing is to make it a habit, as natural as brushing your teeth.

There are many apps now available that provide short meditation practices, and some are free. Why not download one now and give it a try?

Mindfulness is not about emptying your mind; it is about focus and balance. You will always have thoughts floating in and out. That's normal. The main thing is to notice them and remind yourself to refocus on your breath to stay in the here and now.

The bonus is that mindfulness doesn't occur only when you are practising meditation. The effect starts to filter into and influence *all* your thinking across the day, so you become more mindful in everything you do.

It's about being mindful *when you first wake up,* to set your intentions for the day. What do you look forward to for the next 24 hours? What will you achieve? Who will you meet? Where will you go?

...when you eat or drink, noticing your food, the aromas, tastes, and textures.

...your interactions and conversations with others. What do you notice about the other person? What did you hear them say? What do you notice about your responses, your feelings, your actions?

..of the impact you have on another person's world, how you connect, how you relate.

...of your environment, the place you are in, and what else is going on around you.

Mindfulness allows us to just "be". In our frenetic world of "doing", it can be good to simply remind ourselves of this great quote of Neale Donald Walsch: "We are human beings not human doings".

CHAPTER 4

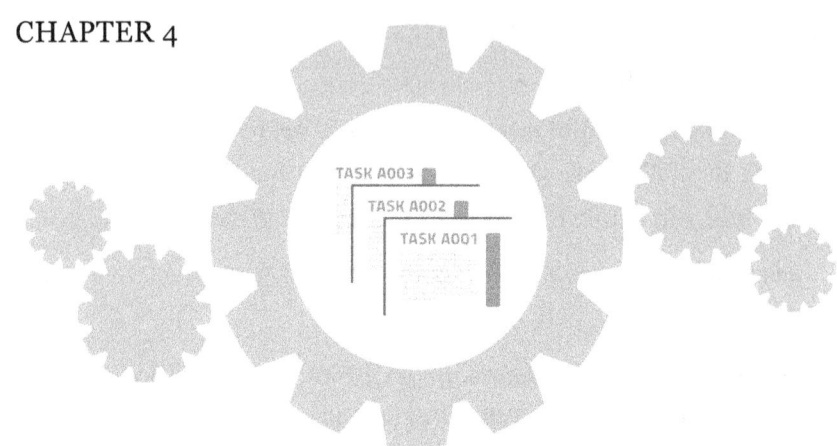

> MANAGING DISTRACTIONS AND MAKING THEM YOUR FRIENDS <

The biggest hurdle for many of us is being able to manage our distractions.

Distractions come in many forms but basically two flavours, internal and external, and it is our internal distractions that interfere *most* with our focus.

Our main internal distractions are daydreaming, mind wandering, and internal chatter with our little voice. What little voice? The one that's talking to you right now. It has the unpleasant tendency to be highly self-critical and negative about our ability to do virtually anything. It's the little voice that doubts that we are doing the right thing or that we are any good, that thinks we probably shouldn't even bother to try because we'll only make a fool of ourselves.

The ability to manage our internal distractions can take a lot of time and perseverance to master. It requires a positive mindset. Psychologist Carol Dweck[38], author of *Mindset*, teaches how we can choose to implement a growth mindset that promotes personal development and a higher level of success across all aspects of our life.

The workplace has been described by some, as being the worst place to work simply because of all the external distractions. Learning how to manage them is crucial to helping make the time for us simply to get on and do our work.

KNOWING YOUR ENEMIES IS CRUCIAL FOR SURVIVAL

The old saying of "Keep your friends close and your enemies closer" is the perfect analogy for our distractions. Recognising the enemy is the prerequisite to taking the appropriate steps to keep them in their place, but it is unrealistic to expect to eliminate them. Life is far too complex for that. It's about taking back control so you are managing your distractions, rather than the other way around.

> "Keep your friends close and your enemies closer."

The time cost of our distractions can be huge, and it's not just about dealing with email. A 2.8-second interruption[39], which could be something as simple as a work colleague popping their head around the door "to ask a quick question", can result in a 24-minute delay and a 50% increase in work errors before you get back to where you were before being interrupted. No wonder so many of us ask ourselves several times a day, "Now, where was I?"

External sources of distraction are easy to recognise. They are

THE COST OF OUR DISTRACTIONS

2.8 SECOND INTERRUPTION + 24 MIN DELAY = 50% INCREASE IN WORK ERRORS

ubiquitous and pervasive, but also sneaky. We may be conscious of their presence, yet sometimes we seem helpless to resist their allure.

So what are they? Emails, phone calls, text messages, meetings, water-cooler conversations, social media, work colleagues, your boss . . . yet the greatest distraction of all, the most damaging and costly (in terms of productivity), is the one we often overlook. The one we simply forget is there all the time. It is ourselves.

Yes, we are the biggest cause of our own distractions. Our self-talk, the conversations we have in our heads with that little voice, prompts endless self-interruption and disrupts our ability to focus. "I don't have a little voice," I hear you thinking. Yes, it's *that* little voice.

One of the problems with our self-talk is that it is predominantly negative. We are often our own biggest critics. If you ever need someone to put the dampeners on a new idea, a dream or a thought, you need look no further than your own negative self-talk. We do it to ourselves all the time. It's so annoying and it can be very damaging.

Some workplaces are described as *work fragmented* because of the number of interruptions endured by the workforce. Studies have shown that in work areas described as *work centric,* staff are interrupted on average every 4 to 11 minutes, and that half of these interruptions are self-initiated.[40] That's right, we cause around 50% of all the distractions we experience on a daily basis.

Paula has been assigned a new project. She is pretty excited about it but not 100% sure of her capability to do an excellent job, because the material is a little outside her usual area. She is worried that if she stuffs up, not only will she look bad but she will be letting the other members of her team down as well.

Sitting in front of her desk, she allocates a couple of hours to start working out a schedule and framework for the project. After ten minutes of staring at a blank screen, she realises she has been thinking more about what could go wrong than what she was being asked to do. She wonders who is around who could help out. Nigel would be good, but he's on leave. Jacinta is excellent technically, but Paula has always found her a little prickly to deal with . . .

She becomes conscious of the fact that her desk is looking pretty messy, so it would be a good idea to straighten that out first, to give herself a clear head and a clear desk so she can work more efficiently. The neat and tidy desk now looks great, but gosh it's 10 o'clock and she needs a coffee to help get her day started . . .

So what can we do to help reduce our self-interruptions, especially when we are required to attend to increasingly complex work that needs our focused attention, problem-solving ability, *and* creativity?

Why do we disappear down those rabbit holes of our own thoughts? Research by Matthew Killingsworth and Daniel Gilbert[41] revealed that we spend 46.9% of our time mind-wandering. So why do we spend so much time in a daydream?

What is actually happening is that we are allowing our executive thinking processes to be activated *alongside* the default system of not paying attention.

Far from being a mindless activity your brain is being highly active. The way to make daydreaming useful is to maintain your meta-awareness, so that if you suddenly come up with a brilliant new idea or way to solve a tricky problem you have been stewing on, you can engage your conscious thought to ensure you quickly make a note to return to later.

So next time you catch yourself drifting off, just check into whether your thoughts are actually on the brink of something really useful.

THE NEWEST BRAIN MYTH KID ON THE BLOCK: MULTITASKING

We all do it: multitask that is. It's everywhere. You see drivers talking on their mobiles (and yes, they know they risk a fine). You see people in the street texting as they walk, often narrowly missing a pole or the traffic. You see people in meetings surreptitiously catching up on their email or working on their laptops. You sit in presentations and realise at least half the audience are tweeting, texting, or asleep.

You have probably been told countless times: multitasking doesn't work, it's dangerous, don't do it. Yet we multitask more and more.

"Houston, we have a problem."

Why? Because we believe we can, because we believe we'll save time, because we believe it allows us to get more stuff done, and *because it makes us feel good*. Getting through our busy days is a challenge on its own. Being able to say to ourselves, "Yes, I've done that, and that, and that!" crossing off all those items on our to-do lists, makes us feel rewarded.

Mulititasking is often perceived as a positive activity, which explains why you see job adverts listing an ability to multitask well (now there's an oxymoron!) as a prerequisite for the position.

Oh dear. I'm sure HR managers and employers are not deliberately looking to take on staff in order to set them up to fail, but sadly that is exactly the outcome when the emphasis is on multitasking. "Houston, we have a problem," and the problem is we are all deluded about our ability to multitask. Research[42] has also shown that those of us who are classed as the most serious serial and chronic multitaskers, are the worst at it and also the most deluded in our perception of our ability!

So before you share the good news with your friends and family, what are our assumptions and what does the brain science tell us about multitasking?

1. We believe our brain is capable of doing anything we ask it to.

Unfortunately, this is not the case. While we do have the most amazing brain, it is not without limitations. You might see this as a design fault; however, *your brain is designed to pay focused attention to one thing and one thing only at a time.*

Which does not mean you cannot do more than one thing at a time. Of course you can. Just don't expect to be paying *focused* attention to any of those items.

Yes, you can prepare dinner, chat with your partner, oversee the kids' homework, and keep half an ear on the evening news. Yes, you can be typing an email while listening to a work colleague telling you about their fun night out last night, and also thinking to yourself you need another coffee. Yes, you can fill in your tax return, while wondering if you remembered to take the chicken out of the freezer to defrost for dinner, and what was it your friend asked you to do for her on Friday? Yet the chances are you won't remember much of what you saw on the news, the conversation you had with your partner, or exactly where it was your friend went out for such a good time.

 MULTITASKING CAUSES US TO REMEMBER LESS OF WHAT WE GIVE OUR DIVIDED ATTENTION TO.

Imagine watching a movie but you can hear only every second or third sentence of the dialogue. You might get the gist, but it's a lot harder to follow and you obviously miss a lot of the detail. Reading the ticker tape of breaking news and headline stories that is shown at the bottom of the TV screen means we take in at least 10% less of the information being shared by the newsreader.

2. We believe it will save us time.

Because we believe we are time poor; finding some way, any way, to help us in our constant battle with time has to be a good thing, doesn't it? We pride ourselves on ticking off items on our to-do list because it gives us a sense of achievement and reward. Our brain craves reward because it triggers the release of dopamine, our feel-good hormone, and once experienced, naturally we want more of that.

Yet because our attention isn't focused on any one thing, our thinking is more scattered and we take longer to finish all those simultaneous jobs than if we prioritised our tasks and did one at a time.

Worse still, we make more mistakes. Far from achieving more in less time, we achieve less as a consequence of taking longer to complete the tasks because we have to correct the unintentional mistakes we made along the way. Studies have shown that multitasking is associated with up to a 50% addition to the time taken to finish our work, and 50% more errors.

Ouch!

3. We believe we are good at it.

This is where the delusion really kicks in. Younger people in particular will often goad the oldies (including parents) over their apparent inability to multitask. Their young, super-efficient brains, on the other hand, are so good at multitasking, right?

Wrong. Younger brains, while faster at processing information, are just as bad at multitasking as everyone else's.

It has to be said that, as with everything else, practice can in some instances make you faster at multitasking, so long as it doesn't matter that you make heaps of mistakes along the way. Whichever way you look at it, multitasking doesn't work.

If you think you are good at something, it's natural to want to continue doing it. Remember though, it's all an illusion. Unless you are one of the 2% of supertaskers in the world who really can divide their attention by using a different part of their brain, the reason you think you are so smart at multitasking is that you are rewarding your brain with your behaviour, and that makes you feel good — it can even become addictive.

Zheng Wang[43], of Ohio State University's School of Communication, explains why so many of us persist in multitasking even though we know it compromises our performance. It is because it makes us feel more emotionally satisfied with the outcome. In one study she asked a group of students to record all their media use and other activity for a 28-day period, why they used different media platforms, and what they thought they got out of it.

Those who watched TV while reading a book reported feeling more emotionally satisfied because they had got on with the task, even while they were aware it didn't help them to achieve their cognitive goals. Feelings matter. If we are entertained while undertaking a task, it makes the whole experience so much more enjoyable. If you like something, then you are likely to want to do it and to continue to do it. Think of it like exercise. You may have decided you need to exercise for your health, but the trick to actually doing it is to find a form of exercise you like and to add a fun element to it.

In another study, she recruited 32 students who agreed to carry a recording device on which they would report on their activities in media use three times a day over a period of three weeks. This included the type of media used (e.g. computer, radio, TV, or print) and the subtype of activity (e.g. surfing the web or social networking). Each activity had to be timed and the students were asked to record whether they were doing any simultaneously. In addition, they had to report their motivation for each task or combination of tasks from a list of seven potential needs, and to rank them.

What she found here was that the students were more likely to multitask if they had a cognitive need, such as they needed to study. Not because it helped their performance (it didn't), but because it met their emotional needs and motivated them to do the task.

She also found that habit plays a large role. The more we get into the habit of multitasking, the more we are likely to continue because we have rewired our brain to create what is called a dynamic feedback loop. If you multitask today, you are much more likely to do it again tomorrow.

The problem here is when people start to feel *compelled* to check their phone multiple times, or believe they can *only* work with the TV on or while listening to music. It isn't helping their performance, but they feel that it does.

Those of us who multitask the most have been found to be more impulsive sensation seekers, overconfident in our ability to multitask but often the worst performers at it. The more we think we are good at it, the more likely we are to be bad at it!

Media multitasking (except using a cell phone while driving) correlates with impulsivity, in particular an inability to concentrate or to act without thinking. Impulsive people are reward seekers, looking for that next quick fix of dopamine. They take more risks, even in the knowledge that this behaviour costs them performance.

How impulsive are you?

WHAT'S WRONG ......WITH OUR BRAIN?

Nothing, except our persistence in trying to get our brain to do something it wasn't designed for.

Focusing your attention engages the part of your prefrontal cortex called the working memory. This is quite a small area of brain, and not only is it small but it is extremely energy hungry, has limited working capacity, and is very fussy about what it will deal with.

You can think of your working memory as like a small stage in a club where there is only room for one leading actor to stand at any one time. While you are engaged with that performer, another actor comes stomping onto the stage, demanding your attention now be focused on him. Then because space is so limited, the only way that can happen is for the first actor to be kicked off. Now you can focus on the second performer. Meanwhile, the first one is scrambling back up to demand that you refocus on him and remove the interloper. This leads to a ping-pong effect as your brain tries to keep all parties happy by switching very quickly from one actor to the other.

This is called dual-task performance. The problem is it chews up an enormous amount of mental energy as your brain goes through the task-switching exercise and rapidly becomes exhausted. It is also time costly. Every time your brain switches from Task A to Task B and back again there is a ten-millisecond interval between being fully disengaged with Task A and fully engaged with Task B. Repeated task switching during the day may cost you up to 40% of your productivity!

Two French neuroscientists, Etienne Koechlin and Sylvain Charron[44], used fMRI scans to look at what goes on in people's brains when they attempt to multitask. The scans revealed that the brain splits the work, with each side of the brain working independently on one of two tasks. This is thought to be the reason why the brain can't handle more than two focused tasks at a time. We don't have enough hemispheres to share the load!

What they also discovered was that trying to add in a third task doesn't work at all, because the brain tosses one of the tasks away completely. Attempting to triple task also led to three times the number of errors caused by dual tasking.

Clifford Nass, Eyal Ophir and Anthony Wagner[45], from Stanford University, undertook a series of experiments to address whether there are systematic differences between chronically heavy and light media multitaskers. They expected to find that those who used multitasking a lot would perform better than the non-multitaskers in at least some of the activities. They were wrong. The chronic multitaskers were bad at all three tasks they were given.

Even when doing only one thing at a time, if you are a chronic multitasker your brain will not perform as well when compared with someone who only ever does one thing at a time. Yes, there are still some people on the planet who work that way!

The studies showed that heavy media multitaskers were more susceptible to interference from irrelevant environmental stimuli and representations in memory, leading to a reduced ability to filter out this interference from the relevant task set.

Being cognitively tired means we take longer to focus on tasks, and attempting to multitask just makes this worse. In dual task interference you experience an actual gap in your cognition, when you are not engaged with Task A *or* Task B. You are not focused on anything at all.

You wouldn't choose to drive your car with a blindfold on for half the time, but that is exactly what we are doing to our brain when we drive and use our phone. Scary thought, isn't it!

No wonder the number of motor vehicle accidents attributed to distracted drivers is so high. It's not just about using our mobile phones when driving either. In the UK, more than 500,000 car accidents have been attributed to female drivers multitasking[46] — putting on their makeup behind the wheel each year. Dr Amy Ship[47] suggests driving while texting (or even talking) is as dangerous as drunk driving. She is very concerned by the proportion of accidents occurring as a consequence of multitasking while driving. In the US, 81% of cell phone owners admit to using them while driving.

I was recently sitting in the back of a taxi whose driver was becoming increasingly irritated by the number of incoming messages and calls on his phone (and I was becoming increasingly nervous!). Eventually, he let out an exasperated sigh and said, "Don't they realise, all this checking in to see where I am, if I've got the next passenger, what the next job is, means it's taking me longer to do my job! Why do they feel they need to be in constant contact all the time?" Why indeed.

The message? You got it. Multitasking is a myth. It scrambles your brain, it's cognitively exhausting, it takes longer to get all your tasks done, and it leads to more errors — hardly an efficiency - productivity boosting exercise.

MULTITASKING STRESSES OUR BRAIN

We are addicted to speed. Our apparent compulsion to work faster, to get more done at an ever-increasing pace, is put down to the constant drive to increase our productivity. Being more productive means a higher output, which for business implies a greater profit, and for the individual more dollars in the pay packet, a better lifestyle, more vacations, and generally more out of life.

Is this reality? Sure, the drive for greater productivity means you are working harder, but are you actually seeing the proposed benefits? Maybe you could, if only you had the time to stop and actually enjoy them.

"Too busy." It's the catch-cry of everyone you speak to, but what is all this busyness doing to our brains? Will we really benefit from this relentless push to go harder and faster?

No.

What we are now witnessing is the impact of this busyness on our cognition and of the addiction that is associated with our love affair with new technologies and multitasking. Being super-busy stresses our brain.

Of course, being busy per se is not bad. Having enough to do to keep yourself occupied in a meaningful way is very rewarding to your brain. It's about knowing the difference between enough work and too much. For some of us being busy is like the never-empty porridge pot. You keep going with your work, but every time you get to the point where you think you can take a break, the pot magically refills itself.

Your prefrontal cortex, the thinking part of your brain, is highly developed, extremely fussy (everything has to be just right for it to function at its optimum) and extremely energy hungry, but it has a limited capacity.

That's right. There's a limit to how much information it can comfortably process at any one time, and because it uses up a lot of energy, mental fatigue can quickly set in if it's overused. The impact of long, stressful days when you feel that there's simply too much to do in the time available is *stress*.

You and your brain can cope with the occasional ridiculously busy day, on a one-off basis. Yet what happens when *every* day is like this: too busy, too much, too fast? It leads to a chronically stressed brain that is cognitively fatigued, underperforming, and at risk of mental distress or illness and burnout. Not a pretty picture, yet how many people do you know who live like this?

The way we live and work, the *how* and the *where*, have changed dramatically in just a few short decades. Your brain has been adapting to change very successfully over millennia. With the pace of change now following an ever steeper trajectory, the questions we need to be asking are, "Can our brains keep up?" and "What do we need to do differently to ensure our continuing success?"

We are all different, as is our capacity and resilience to different stressors, so there is no simple, one-size-fits-all answer. Though because you have a plastic brain capable of rewiring itself, you can use your natural plasticity to enhance those new skills and habits that will ensure your continuing ability to adapt to and keep up with rapid change.

Yet there's more at stake. It has been recognised that for many of us the impact of our technology on our thinking needs to be addressed, to ensure we are not actually asking our brain to work in a way it was not designed for. Otherwise, we risk overloading our brain circuits with stuff that hampers our mental stamina and cognitive powers.

MULTITASKING AFFECTS PERFORMANCE

The impact of multitasking has to be viewed from two perspectives — that of the individual and of business.

Dave has just settled in to attend to an important piece of work that *has* to be completed by the end of the day. Opening up the task sheet, he decides to quickly check his emails to ensure he hasn't missed anything important. A flurry of emails, some with red flags, downloads into his inbox, and after a quick skim he determines to answer a couple of the most urgent ones while listening to his voicemail.

In the midst of composing a long and complex email, there is a knock on his door and a colleague pokes her head around the corner to ask if he could just give her a minute, and by the way, there's a phone call for him from the States. As he acknowledges this, he completes the email and accidentally presses the Delete button instead of Send. As his colleague leaves the office, she reminds Dave about the team meeting scheduled for this morning, which is due to start in ten minutes.

Ten minutes later, he is sitting in the conference room wondering why half the team haven't appeared. The meeting starts late. The convenor hasn't prepared all the pertinent documents and a heated discussion begins between several of the staff. Dave decides to use the time whilst they sort things out to think about his work, which he still hasn't started, and opens up his laptop.

A thought pops into his head about the conversation he had yesterday with a friend about that new restaurant he had tried. He decides to have a quick look at the website to check out the reviews. Someone in the meeting then directs a question to him about an item on the agenda, but because he hasn't been following the conversation his reply is off target.

Back in his office, Dave decides that time is getting on so he had better defer lunch until he has made at least some progress on the main task of the day.

Sound familiar?

The problem with this scenario is the cost to the individual in terms of productivity, energy and time. *One Flew Over the Cuckoo's Nest*, with Jack Nicholson, was a great movie, but does your work ever make you feel as if you are going slowly insane? Learning how to juggle is a great cross-training activity for the brain, but trying to juggle too many balls at once in our work capacity invariably causes us to drop one, if not all of them!

One of the reasons we are spending longer at work is because we are trying to do too many things at once. It doesn't work. You end up cognitively and physically exhausted, and if this is a regular pattern you are putting yourself at increasing risk of your stress levels leading to physical illness, anxiety, or depression.

Your brain was not designed to spend long periods of time paying highly focused attention. Nor was it designed to work in a fragmented way. Getting productivity up, stress levels down, and a sense of achievement recovered *can* be achieved by adopting some strategies to help you and your brain work more effectively together. Let's consider some of the information available to us about work fragmentation in relation to emails and stress.

Gloria Mark[48] and her associates have examined how our work is fragmented and by what. Many people now work in an environment in which multiple interruptions occur across the entire day. For example, it is estimated that the average information worker is interrupted approximately every three minutes. These are people employed to spend their time creating, developing, sharing, and consuming information. Gloria and her team have reported that the number of times we interrupt ourselves depends on our working environment. Those working in open-plan offices will self-interrupt at a higher rate, and more often as a result of personal work needs, while many of our external distractions are due to centralised work that we do with others.

It will take you an average of 64 seconds simply to open up an email and determine whether or not it requires a quick response. Multiply that by several hundred and you quickly start to get a sense of where some of that precious time is disappearing. In some instances, just dealing with emails has been reported to take up 23 to 28% of the total working day. No wonder it can feel as if there's not enough time to do everything else.

In 2012 Gloria[49] and her team undertook a small study in which email access to a group of workers was cut off for five days. The results showed that without email people multitasked less, had a longer task focus, and had lower levels of stress, as measured by heart rate variability.

TAKING BACK CONTROL OF YOUR INBOX

You may or may not be a in a position to reduce email use in your own work situation. However, there are a couple of strategies that might help to make a difference.

1. **Determine your own schedule** for opening and responding to emails during the workday. For example, it could be three times a day — once in the morning, once at lunchtime, and once at the end of the day.

    Many people start their workday by checking their emails. This is generally *not* recommended. Firstly, you are using some of your most valuable and productive thinking time, which would be better spent thinking about those tasks that require a higher level of cognition. Secondly, getting at least one important thing done first will reward your brain, leading to a dopamine surge that promotes a sense of satisfaction, a better mood, and the motivation to get on well with the rest of your day.

2. **Establish a time limit** for how long you will devote to email. If you have only 20 minutes, you may be surprised by how quickly you can determine what needs attention and what doesn't, and can therefore respond in a shorter time frame.

3. **Resist the temptation** to send out group or cc emails. Often the information the email contains is pertinent to only one person, so why bombard everyone else with information they don't need?

4. **Add a message to your email signature** advising that you check your email at certain times of the day and that if the message is urgent the sender should contact you by phone or send a text message. Educating your colleagues is part of helping reduce email overload. Sharing information can be so fast that we often fall into the trap of treating an email as if we are actually speaking to that person. So if we don't get an instant response, we feel slighted or upset. The reality is that your recipient may simply be busy doing something else at the time. It's about treating each other with respect.

5. **Get professional help.** Yes, there are email consultants at hand who can help you develop a strategy that will put you firmly back in charge of your inbox. Jani Murphy[50] is a specialist in the area of information overload and has had many years of experience helping individuals and businesses to regain control of their email.

WE LOVE OUR SOCIAL MEDIA

The statistics on social media usage reveal our love affair with this modern technology. Thanks to Craig Smith[51] from expandedramblings.com who compiled the following statistics (which he updates regularly on his website):

SOCIAL MEDIA USERS

| 1.11 BILLION | 500 MILLION | 225 MILLION | 1 BILLION |

As of June 2013 there were over 1.11 billion Facebook users around the world, with 665 million users active daily.

Twitter, which burst into life in 2006, now has 500 million users. China has the greatest number of twitterers — 35.5 million.

LinkedIn, launched in 2003 and therefore one of the older social networks, now has over 225 million users covering 200 countries and territories.

Then of course there's YouTube, which currently has one billion users and 4 billion views per day.

There's a lot of activity out there. So do you Facebook, Tweet or Link In? Do you have your own YouTube channel? How is this impacting on your work, your life, and your relationships?

THE STORY SO FAR ABOUT BRAINS AND TECHNOLOGY ADDICTION

The issue of technology dependence and addiction is now being extensively investigated and reported on because of some indications of negative impacts.

How often are you checking into your Facebook account, Twitter, or your mobile phone? We do this because our social brain likes to "feel" connected with others. We like the dopamine reward our brain experiences when we share a contact, message, or picture; and we don't want to miss out on something that could be exciting or novel.

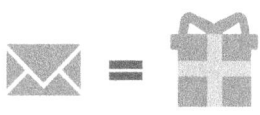

WE ARE INSATIABLY CURIOUS CREATURES AND EVERY UNOPENED EMAIL, TEXT, OR UPDATE IS LIKE AN UNOPENED PRESENT UNDER THE CHRISTMAS TREE.

We are insatiably curious creatures and every unopened email, text, or update is like an unopened present under the Christmas tree. We want to open all of them, and right now. Do we really *need* to check in so frequently? Consider some of the findings from surveys looking at smart phone use:

- One in five people report checking their mobile phone for updates every 10 minutes. Some check their phones 36 times every hour.
- Seventy-five per cent of mobile phone users take them to bed — and no, it's not just to use them as an alarm clock.
- Thirty per cent of mobile phone users admit to using them in the bathroom. Eeeew!
- Forty-six per cent of mobile phone users use them while eating with family around the dinner table.
- Forty per cent of mobile phone users admit to experiencing some level of withdrawal symptoms if they can't get access to their phone.

- Sixty per cent of people report that they wished they didn't feel quite so compelled to check for updates.

What is the first thing you do every morning when you wake up? Is it a trip to the loo or to put the kettle on? Or is it checking the time and your emails/texts/messages on your phone — even before you have got your feet out onto the bedroom floor?

SMARTPHONE USERS

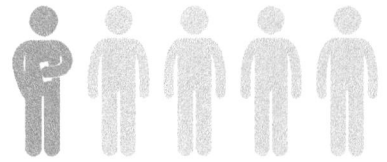

CHECK THEIR MOBILE PHONE FOR UPDATES EVERY 10 MINUTES

TAKE THEM TO BED

USE THEM IN THE BATHROOM

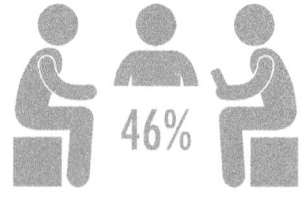

USE THEM WHILE EATING WITH THE FAMILY AROUND THE DINNER TABLE

ADMIT TO EXPERIENCING SOME LEVEL OF WITHDRAWAL SYMPTOMS IF THEY CAN'T GET ACCESS TO THEIR PHONE

WISHED THEY DIDN'T FEEL QUITE SO COMPELLED TO CHECK FOR UPDATES.

Mobile phones are part and parcel of our work artillery. It's not that we don't want to have them available, but we do need some semblance of control over when and where they are used.

I've heard some people say they wish their smart phone was just a phone! I'm sure you can still buy those, but maybe it's an indication that their phone use is not in balance. Having a smart phone that provides so much additional information — a communication channel for important messages using a variety of different media, a clock, a diary, a reminder service, a calculator, a music library, a compass, maps, so many apps — is wonderful.

We recognise our phones are a nuisance when they ring while we are trying to focus our attention on something else, or when they disturb others in meetings, presentations, and even conversation. Convention today is that we start meetings and workshops with the request that everyone turns off their mobile phone. Unfortunately, sometimes we may think we did, only to discover, redfaced, that we didn't, or we forgot to turn it back to silent mode after a coffee break.

Seventy-five per cent of Americans admit to using their cell phones at work for non-work related matters. This may simply reflect the increasingly blurry line between work time and non-work time, after "normal" work hours, when business expects staff to remain contactable by phone or email. These non-work activities include looking for another job, visiting online dating sites, researching medical problems, or shopping online for clothes.

Responding to a phone call or text message while at work can of course have serious implications from a health and safety point of view. There have been several instances of cell phone related death or injury because the person's involuntary reflex to answer the phone or send a text message distracted them. This is, of course, of particular importance in a work area where machinery with moving parts is being operated.

Some workplaces have instigated social media policies to ensure everyone's safety, or simply to reduce the amount of time workers are distracted by personal or other calls. Conversely, other workplaces have supplied their staff with phones, laptops and tablets to keep them in constant contact.

A study of over 2500 people published by Wistia[52] in 2011 found that 64% of Americans use the workplace to watch online videos; 25% of the videos related to news clips and 17% were work-related videos. So not all workplace video watching is of repeat episodes of *Family Guy,* or funny bleating goats. Of those trying to hide their behaviour, 64% admitted to hiding a mobile device under a desk or table, 42% went to the bathroom (a long bathroom break!) and 35% hid their smart phone or tablet in a folder on their desk.

What policy does your workplace have in regard to phone usage and social media?

TIPS FOR MAINTAINING PHONE AND SOCIAL MEDIA SANITY

1. **Turn off push notifications** in the social networks you use and your email inbox. That means you don't get that stimulus of every ping or ring when you receive an update or text. You get to choose the time you do your checking in. Sounds obvious, I know, but have you done it?

2. Determine the times that best suit your schedule to switch off your phone or laptop. Some people decide that after 5 pm they don't answer mobile calls related to work. Others decide they will not use their computer or check their email after 7 pm. You can block in short segments of time when you will attend to email and messages.

There are various online tools to manage your access to email or the web, including Strict Pomodoro, Inbox Pause, and Notify Me Not.

3. Video games are often used as a form of relaxation, and there's nothing wrong with that. There are a lot of pluses to using video games. They improve your reaction time, speed of processing information, and ability to take in the bigger picture while focused. People who play these games a lot have greater manual dexterity which can be very useful, for example, for a surgeon. Studies have shown that the surgeons best suited to perform laparoscopic procedures are not necessarily those with the most clinical experience; they are those who play video games.

For this reason video games are used to enhance driving skills, particularly in those groups recognised as being at the greatest risk of motor vehicle accidents — the youngest drivers on our roads (under 25) and our seniors.

Yet have you had friends with kids, or heard of families, whose experience of video games is of an addiction that is tearing the family apart? Adult or child, a person can become so addicted that they no longer participate in normal family life and activities. In extreme cases, they may choose not to eat or sleep because of the demands of the game.

Maybe it's time to check in and ask yourself a couple of questions:

- Do you ever feel you spend too much time on the Internet outside normal work requirements?
- Do you spend 38 hours a week or more online?
- If the Internet or your smart phone is not available, do you experience "withdrawal symptoms"?
- Do you find you have to spend longer to get the same "high" from playing online games?
- Have you lost interest in your other hobbies or relationships?
- Have you tried unsuccessfully to curb your use?
- Do you use the Internet as a means of escape?

Taiwan is a country admired for its manufacturing productivity and advanced digital technology, but the Taiwanese are also having to deal with a level of Internet addiction that far outweighs what we have so far witnessed here in Australia. It has been estimated that up to 10% of the teenage population has a significant Internet addiction. It has become such a serious problem that there are now more than 240 clinics and a number of hospital wards devoted to the management of the condition. The "norm" for Internet use for gaming in Taiwan is six hours a day. Internet Addiction Disorder is diagnosed when individuals spend 17 hours a day online.

In the US, Internet addiction is now recognised as affecting more individuals than gambling addiction.

In the US, Internet addiction is now recognised as affecting more individuals than gambling addiction.

When you consider that the average person spends 8.5 hours a day in front of a computer screen, it is easy to see how quickly we have adapted in the short time frame that computers, laptops, and smart phones have been available to us. It is now hard to imagine working without these tools, and you probably don't want to, but the best way to help maintain your attention span and other cognitive function is, firstly, to be aware of how much time you are spending online and participating in other social media activities and, secondly, to devise a plan to keep it all in balance. Feeling sufficiently socially connected can sometimes conflict with getting our work done.

ORGANISATIONS AND MULTITASKING

Much of the discussion on the impact of multitasking has been around the effect on individual health and performance, but of course it has a significant impact on organisations as a whole, where the effect of multitasking becomes multiplied.

People don't work in silos. They work within business communities, contributing their work to a team effort or particular project. Often their contribution will depend on another person's input. A delay by one member of the team can have a domino effect on everyone. This can be the impact of collective multitasking.

How often have you experienced the frustration of working very hard to meet a deadline, then realising you can't complete your work because you are waiting for a document from another colleague, who is the only source of some essential data?

Their own issues with getting their work out on time may relate to the different distractions and multitasking they are experiencing. The consequence is that, because you have a million and one other tasks waiting to be done, you start doing something else.

In the brain we have to synchronise the various neuronal networks to form attention. It's the same in the workplace. Synchrony across the organisation is essential for workplace performance and the bottom line.

Managers who fall into the multitasking trap may feel increasingly time poor. They may be managing twenty, forty, or one hundred people. If they are trying to juggle too many things, the time they have available for putting out the next spot fire is limited. Which is why team members can feel frustrated if they sense their manager isn't "with" them. If you have an issue or concern or are simply seeking clarification, a cursory two-minute conversation with your manager, who may not even stop what else they are doing while having that conversation with you, is less likely to result in a happy ending.

So what can businesses and organisations do to reduce multitasking in the workplace? Can multitasking in teams be approached in a different way — as a collaborative activity?

In 2010 Gloria Mark and Hideto Yuzawa[53] developed a prototype to help people manage their interruptions by advising others in their team of their availability for interruptions on specific projects. They based this on their premise that multitasking is a collaborative activity, because task switching will often affect our interdependencies with other team-mates. How we prioritise our tasks and how we determine when to respond to an email or interrupt someone else may require negotiation between all collaborating parties. They called their prototype the Japanese Garden — based on Japanese rock gardens, which are highly stylised and use raked sand to evoke feelings of tranquillity and rocks to evoke contemplation, which in the prototype represent a person's different projects.

How we prioritise, allocate time, and interrupt ourselves or others is often completely independent of how others may be operating. Task switching is time-consuming and inefficient. What if your workplace had a system in place that allowed you to tell others if you are available to be spoken to or contacted about one particular project, and at the same time to see that your colleague Mary will be free at midday to discuss another project you are working on, while Tony, who is dealing with a different task, will not be available until after 4 pm?

The beauty of this system is that it simplifies the whole process and, once learned, removes some of the associated stress of trying to handle multiple projects with others who are working to different timetables and agendas. Results so far suggest that using a technique such as the Japanese Garden can be useful. The researchers indicate this can be viewed as a first step in examining how task management can support collaborative work on multiple tasks.

AVOIDING MULTITASKING IN THE WORKPLACE

1. **Build awareness among all staff** of why multitasking doesn't work — because even the brain has its limits.

2. **Don't reward multitasking!** If you are asking your staff to multitask you are asking them to fail, so why do it? Look to reward your brain in a different way. Giving up an addictive habit is hard. Just ask anyone who has tried to give up smoking. It doesn't have to be a huge reward, just something that makes you feel good. It's all about allowing your brain to experience that little dopamine rush from such simple things as:

    (a) getting home on time

    (b) being able to take a full lunch break — *outside* the office

    (c) being part of an incentive scheme: a reward for higher productivity, public acknowledgement, or a token of appreciation for working smarter.

3. **Encourage a work culture in which** meetings are held in a mobile/laptop-free zone. Obviously, this will depend on the nature of work being done, but the aim is to keep the focus on the agenda items only.

4. **Introduce technology-free zones or breaks;** for example, an email-free Wednesday morning or an Internet-free zone on Thursdays. Depending on the workplace and culture, transitioning to more face-to-face communication may help reduce the number of interruptions that are assumed to require an instant response.

    Focusing hard on a particular task requires your *full* attention. So why not choose the time and space that best suits you to hang up a "Do not disturb" or "Brain at work — come back later" sign and shut the office door. Turn off your mobile phone and shut down your email alert system. Tell your colleagues/PA/telephone receptionist you are unavailable for X amount of time.

5. **Sequencing your tasks** at the end of the day or before you start your work in the morning allows you to map out the important tasks and their order of priority. Like playing Monopoly, it's about moving steadily forward, a few steps at a time, and not being allowed to pass GO until the first task is completed. Your brain is at its freshest first thing, so ideally that's the time to tackle the more complex thinking tasks. Getting the order right for which jobs to do first can save a lot of precious time, energy, and effort.

6. **Take on fewer projects.** This may appear to be organisational suicide. However, resisting the temptation to say yes to all new work allows you to allocate more time to ensuring that existing work is done well, with fewer errors, and inside the deadline. Overcommitment helps no one, and especially not yourself. Research has shown that reducing the total number of work projects by 25 to 50% can double completion rates!

7. **Follow the OHIO rule**: Only Handle It Once.

8. **Prioritise**, distinguishing the urgent from the important and everything else needing to be done. If the company policy is to firstly address those tasks that have been clearly identified and communicated as taking priority, then everyone is on the same page. It distinguishes then those items that can be allocated to a different time.

9. **Provide total clarity** about what is required and expected before a new project is started. This is about ensuring all staff involved in a project know exactly what they are required to do as well as the other specifications relating to the work. Certainty provides clarity, which leads to confidence of execution. A certain brain is also a less stressed brain, which means it is capable of achieving more.

10. **Automate** some of the tasks you are required to do.

    Over the course of our day, much of our thoughts and activities are repeats. Watching re-reruns of *Days of Our Lives* has nothing on the constant repetition our subconscious brain works in getting us through our daily work. Much of the time we run on autopilot, because we don't need to engage our conscious brain on routine tasks; it's too cognitively demanding. Our subconscious does a lot of the donkeywork, so you don't have to think how you brush your teeth, button up a shirt, use a computer mouse, or even drive your car.

    Creating habits means that the basal ganglia, your mental warehouse of habits and routines, can take up the load and free up your prefrontal cortex for more important thinking. You can achieve this easily; it just requires practice.

11. **Introduce a positive technique**, such as the Japanese Garden, using collaboration of individuals working in teams to reduce the number of coordination messages and interruptions.

12. **Limit time spent on tasks using divided attention.** If you know you are going to be spending some time dividing your attention between tasks, then set a time limit. Reducing cognitive fatigue is all about awareness and spacing.

CAN MULTITASKING EVER BE TRAINED?

If you want to get faster at multitasking, yes you can train yourself to do this. Research from Vanderbilt University[54] found that cognitive training increases brain processing speed and our speed of multitasking. However, getting faster is not correlated with any improvement in efficiency and productivity. The old saying, more haste less speed, is the perfect analogy for multitasking. The faster you multitask, the more mistakes you make. So why would you even try?

The researchers found that practice led to improvement in how fast the brain processed the information, *but* the brain was still experiencing dual task interference. So you can learn to multitask faster — you just stay bad at it.

There are groups of professionals and employees who *enjoy* a multitasking environment. There is nothing these groups like more than the thrill and the buzz of having lots of things on simultaneously. They thrive on it! The thinking is that if such individuals and groups can be identified, they may be especially suited to certain work environments where a higher resilience to multitasking is not only the norm but is required. Think air traffic controllers, emergency operators, taxi drivers, even receptionists. Some psychologists are now trying to ascertain a tool to identify which people will thrive in different work environments, which may help for better future staff selection and retention.

CHAPTER 5

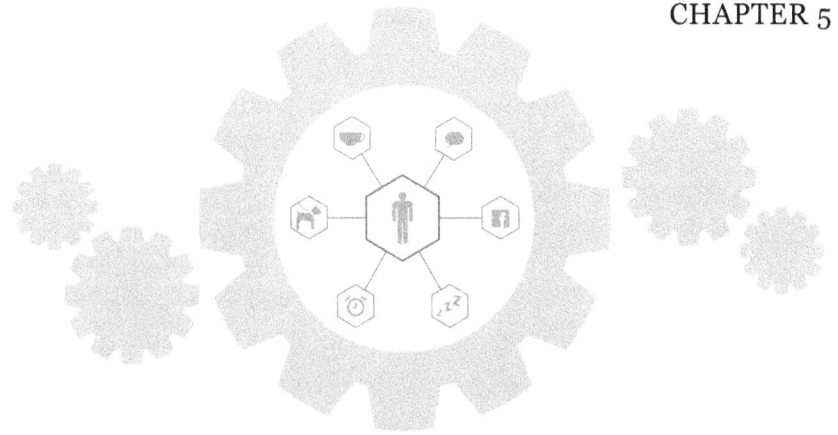

PROCRASTINATE: WHY DO WE?

I read recently that many more people enrol in a PhD program than ever complete it, which seems a real shame considering the amount of time and effort that goes into the study required.

I experienced this first hand recently during a Post Graduate Certificate course I had enrolled in. The course was quite expensive and demanded a considerable commitment to the work. We had weekly 90-minute webinars, fortnightly pod-calls lasting around an hour, and extensive reading lists. We were required to produce a number of fully referenced essays, in addition to undertaking a research project. The time commitment was 18 months to two years. This was on top of any other fulltime work, of course.

During the course we were constantly reminded of the submission deadlines for our final essays and assignments. The university took no prisoners, and anyone who was so much as five minutes late would be deemed a "no-show". We were on the final home straight when one of the course organisers shared with us the news that two students in the group ahead of us had missed the deadline and therefore forfeited the opportunity to complete their certificate. I couldn't believe it. Why, after all that time, all that effort, did they fall at the last hurdle? Did they misread the time? Did they oversleep? Did their server go into meltdown five minutes before the deadline? I'll never know. One reason, however, may have been that they simply fell foul of procrastination.

Time and again I see the same story play out: what distinguishes one person from another in how successful they are, isn't their level of intelligence, their social background, their contacts, or how much money they have. It's not even luck.

It boils down to the difference between those who procrastinate and those who don't. The person who succeeds is the person who steps up, who initiates and does the work, including the tough and the boring stuff. Countless studies have shown that success is less about talent and more about overcoming procrastination.

WHAT IS PROCRASTINATION?

Procrastination is an irrational behaviour. It is the deliberate putting off or delaying of tasks, which we understand leaves us worse off than if we completed them sooner. The word is derived from the Latin *Crastinus*, meaning "of tomorrow", and *pro*, meaning "in favour of" or "forward".

What we also know is that this irrational behaviour, which can drive so many of us crazy, is rooted in our evolution and is consequently a behaviour that is deeply ingrained.

"The early bird catches the worm" is an adage first recorded in the 17th century. Mark Twain's more whimsical advice was, "Never put off until tomorrow what you can do the day after tomorrow". Though before declaring your admiration for early birds or Mark Twain, have you considered the sorts of tasks you might be tempted to procrastinate over? Could it be that new article you have to write, that important tender to prepare, or that difficult phone call waiting to be made?

What are some of the thoughts we use to allow ourselves to put things off?

- I'm not in the right mood.
- I have to find the right time.
- I don't have enough time.
- I've just got to [insert choice of activity: make coffee/put the washing on/feed the dog/fold the laundry] first.
- I don't have the energy.
- My boss/Aunt Mabel/partner/best mate has asked for my help with something else right now.

Don't feel too bad, because you are not alone with this affliction. It has been estimated that 95% of us procrastinate to a greater or lesser degree. That suggests there is an awful lot of pain being experienced around missed potential or lost opportunities as a consequence.

Naturally, there will be times when it makes sense to defer a task. Just because you have an important work document to send out doesn't mean you do that rather than attend to another crisis or emergency simply because you don't want to be seen to be procrastinating. Nor is it bad to take time off to relax and enjoy yourself.

Piers Steele[55], author of *The Procrastination Equation* and a world expert on what makes us procrastinate, reminds us that chronic procrastination is not a time management problem; it's an impulse control problem. Nor is it simply to do with being a perfectionist. In fact, perfectionists have been shown to be less likely to procrastinate. Although this rule is not absolute!

My good friend Dr Jason Fox[56], an expert in helping people design work to be inherently motivating, uses a lovely term, *Procrastifection*, which seductively couples a perfectionistic trait with a procrastinating tendency. This is something I have recognised on many occasions in myself, which may reflect the fact that perfectionists can sometimes get a bit obsessive about getting everything done right regardless of how much love and attention needs to be applied to every single detail.

So it's not that we lack the intention to do the work. We simply find other, less important tasks that need doing first. Which is why you clean out the kitchen cupboards instead of putting in those extra couple of hours studying for an exam.

We pay a personal cost for our procrastinating habits. We all have the ability to procrastinate; it's just that some of us have got it down to a fine art, and it hurts. Have you asked yourself how much your procrastination is holding you back in terms of your career prospects, your financial situation, your health and wellbeing, even your level of happiness?

Our proclivity to procrastinate not only annoys us; it also affects those around us who witness our behaviour. Yet it is just behaviour, and like any other habit it can be changed, because of your wonderful plastic brain.

Some of the main reasons we procrastinate are:
- **Boredom:** The task doesn't excite us in any way.
- **Overwhelm:** The task seems too huge or too far outside our comfort zone to know where to start.
- **Fatigue:** When we are tired it's that much harder to summon the enthusiasm and energy to do what is required.
- **Distraction:** We allow ourselves to be diverted by the million and one other things on our to-do list.
- **The task lacks value:** If it's not something we believe will be of use to us, why bother? There are plenty of other tasks we could be doing instead.

HARDWIRED TO PROCRASTINATE

Our brain evolved to keep us safe, which led us to become impulsive. This may sound counterintuitive, but understanding our impulsive nature makes it easier to understand why we procrastinate, and how best then to manage our dithering nature.

As hunter-gatherers 9000 years ago, it made sense to catch food if it walked past and to eat it immediately so as to prevent any other hungry beast from taking it. It made sense to take shelter when you found it, especially if the elements were threatening. It also made sense to mate when the opportunity presented itself, to ensure the group's survival and continuation.

Hence impulsivity has been an essential part of human nature. The reason why so many of us appear hardwired to procrastinate is that we are often impulsive. Are you one of those people who love to rush in and buy those new shoes you just saw in the shop window, or who purchases everything based on "special" deals, or who gets really excited by all the latest electronic gadgets and gizmos?

So why does being impulsive mean we procrastinate? Because our impulsivity means we accept the short term gratification of buying the new shoes or outfit at the expense of our longer term goal, which is to save up for a new car.

Over the course of our evolution, we humans developed larger forebrains, a neocortex capable of thinking about our thoughts. It provided a means by which to compare and evaluate information, allowing us to make better decisions, to plan and to pay strategic attention to what we consider important.

As already discussed, this newer part of the brain provides us with the powers of reason, analysis and logic. However, the drawback of this new system is that it operates more slowly, is easily fatigued, and has a limited working capacity. Another part of our brain, the older limbic system associated with emotions and their regulation, is by contrast very fast and strong.

Despite the shortcomings of the neocortex, the two systems, fast and slow, work together to regulate the rather jumpy emotional part of the brain. This works fine until additional factors upset this delicate balance, such as those times when we experience stress.

Stress upsets the balance between instinct and reason and favours the faster, stronger limbic system. Which is why it is so much harder to do those things you don't really want to do when you are tired, lacking in energy, or feeling overwhelmed. Our stressed response is to say, "I'll do that tomorrow" or "I'll deal with that later".

Sometimes it can be prudent to call it quits when you are tired, rather than persist and risk producing lower quality work. Brains do tire easily. Knowing the right time to take a break, to refuel and keep going is the key. Failing to heed the warning signs of impending fatigue, hunger or emotion is what leads to loss of momentum, and coming back the next time to finish off just got a whole lot harder.

Intention and procrastination are not good bedfellows. Your intention was to finish doing all the background reading before starting a new assignment, but your favourite TV reality show was on, and it was the grand finale. Your intention was to empty your inbox by the end of the week and implement the new efficient system for handling all your messages and important documents, but you had a lot of other important work that had to be done and you never got around to your email. Your intention was to sign up for that great new course that would provide you with the opportunity to improve your chances of promotion, but you forgot to check the cut-off date for applications and missed out.

WILLPOWER: SHARING OUR BUCKET OF SELF CONTROL

Walter Mischel's famous marshmallow experiment[57] from 1972 is a lovely illustration of how the ability to defer gratification, or self-control (developed by the tender age of four), can help determine the success you enjoy in your life. His experiment showed that the more impulsive we are, the harder it is to delay the reward our brain is seeking. In other words, the more impulsive our nature, the more inclined we are to procrastinate.

Offering four-year-olds the choice between getting one marshmallow straight away, or waiting to get two marshmallows, showed how those with the greatest self-control used a variety of different strategies to distract their attention from the desired object. For example, they would look elsewhere around the room or tap their fingers on the table to avoid looking at the marshmallow sitting right in front of them. A positive form of distraction!

Those who were more impulsive were simply unable to resist and ate the marshmallow right away. The full implication of this was revealed some years later on a follow-up[58] of those children who had taken part in the test as four-year-olds. Those who obtained the highest SAT scores for college were those who had exerted the greatest degree of self-control.

Putting in the effort to study hard and sit multiple exams to qualify for a university degree, seeing your friends being paid for their work, and going out and socialising while you are stuck at home revising, requires commitment and a large dollop of self-control. It is this ability to push on through the hard stuff to reach the greater prize that makes many of us choose to take up the challenge. Without it we would not see people decide to climb Mount Everest, or strive to become a leader, a manager, or CEO.

This is one of the elements that psychologist Martin Seligman[59],

> Willpower is not something we are necessarily endowed with in huge quantities, and because our bucket of willpower has to be shared among *all* our cognitive tasks over the course of a day, it can easily be exhausted.

who wrote the great book *Flourish*, sees as essential to providing us with the ability not just to do well, but to flourish in all aspects of our lives. We need that element of "grit".

Willpower is not something we are necessarily endowed with in huge quantities, and because our bucket of willpower has to be shared among *all* our cognitive tasks over the course of a day, it can easily be exhausted. Which is why if you have spent your day putting out spot fires, making lots of decisions and choosing not to do certain things, then by evening your willpower bucket may be pretty much empty. So resisting that slice of chocolate cake after dinner is so much harder than it would have been at 10 o'clock in the morning.

The good news though, is that willpower, like attention, can be exercised like a muscle[60] and increased with practice. So don't despair if you recognise that your tendency to be impulsive makes you more prone to procrastination.

LEARNING TO OVERCOME OUR PROCRASTINATING TENDENCIES

There are a number of elements that can contribute to our proclivity to procrastinate. The first of these is the result of when we are faced with too many choices. Another is the value we ascribe to the particular task at hand.

THE PARADOX OF TOO MUCH CHOICE

It's good to have choices. Your brain feels a lot safer when you have the security of autonomy, and a safe brain is more open to considering all the options and alternatives available to it. Except that, paradoxically, too much choice can lead to a paralysis of indecision and procrastination. If the decision is too hard, you will either defer making a decision at all (sometimes a wise move) or just choose something, anything, simply to get the decision out of the way so you can move on.

Psychologist Barry Schwartz[61], author of *The Paradox of Choice*, suggests that too much choice contributes to decision paralysis and causes unhappiness. He described the famous jam study in which one group of subjects could choose to buy a jar after sampling from an array of 24 different types of high-quality exotic jams. The second group were offered a choice of just six jams to sample, although the entire array was available to purchase. The results showed that only 3% of the subjects offered the entire range of jams purchased a jar, whereas 30% of the group offered the smaller sample range bought a jar.

Have you ever had this experience? It could be picking the best applicant for a new position from a large field of applicants with similar CVs and experience. It could be choosing which new idea to implement from all those great ones thrown out in your team brainstorming session. Or it could simply be choosing which jar of peanut butter to buy from the supermarket — crunchy, smooth, or just a hint of crunch?

GETTING THE VALUE RIGHT

One reason we procrastinate is the lack of value we ascribe to the task at hand. Here we may have to look at the task and ask ourselves, "How much does this matter to me?" For example, if the task required is going to earn you big brownie points in terms of status or a significant bonus, that may be of higher value than just the reward of ticking it off on the "done" board.

Peter had struggled with his weight for most of his life. Fast approaching the wrong side of forty, he was aware that he was almost at the same age as when his father had his first heart attack. (His dad had died of coronary artery disease in his early fifties.) Not only that but he was in a sedentary job, spending most of his waking hours sitting in front of a computer screen, and while he tried to make the right dietary choices, he was easily tempted by a packet of chips when his energy levels were running low.

He had often thought about joining a weight loss program or seeing a dietician, but he had never put a high enough value on his own health to get around to making an appointment.

If you recognise that the value you ascribe to your task is low, how can you find a way to reframe your perception so as to *add* value and reduce your impulse to procrastinate? If, like Peter, you want to lose weight and get fit, the value to you may be in feeling energised and well. You could look to elevate this value further, for example, by deciding to participate in and complete a half marathon in six months' time. Now the value bar has been raised and it will be far easier to overcome all those reasons why you haven't yet taken the first steps.

PROCRASTINATION HAS ALL THE ELEMENTS OF A GOOD STORY.

How we procrastinate varies from person to person and task to task. Sometimes though we can recognise a bit of a pattern and this is what allows you the opportunity to work on which strategy is best likely to help you overcome the problem.

All good stories will incorporate three elements:

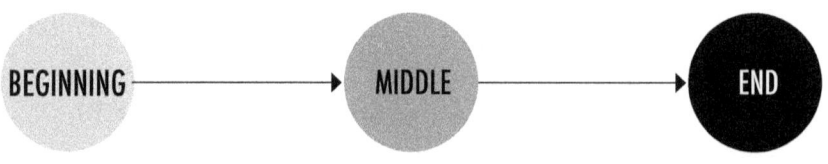

Procrastinators can find themselves getting stuck in any one of these.

PROCRASTINATION AND GETTING STARTED.

Some people find it extraordinarily hard to start a new task. For writers who complain of "writer's block" the inspiration to craft a story or an article seems to have simply flown out of the window, for hours, days, or even weeks on end. It can be incredibly frustrating to find yourself staring at a blank computer screen or at a blank sheet of paper that simply can't get any meaningful words written on it. The pressure of not starting alerts our limbic system of the brain, which recognises that the stress response is being activated. The more you stress about not starting, the more you are self-sabotaging your chance of getting going.

Fear of starting can also be aligned with other fears, including fear of failure and fear of success. These are often "what-if scenarios":

- *What if* I do it wrong?
- *What if* others see me do it wrong?
- *What if* I get it right and then more is expected of me?
- *What if* it's just not good enough?

Which can lead to "What if I ignore it for long enough — will it go away?"

If you are a non-starter and recognise this is the key area holding you back, your first task is to identify what is it about this task that is causing you to procrastinate in this way, and then to do something about it. There are a number of things that you can do.

1. Look at the size of the project

A big task can lead to a sense of overwhelm. This can have the same effect on your brain as the paradox of too much choice. If this is the case, try to break it down into smaller, more manageable chunks and start one of these. If inspiration doesn't come with the first chunk, try another, even smaller one — one that you have the greatest confidence in achieving. It's not about looking for perfection or a final outcome; it's simply a means to get started.

My friend Lesley writes articles, and she writes very well, but sometimes she gets stuck and can't think of the right way to start. So rather than sitting there getting increasingly frustrated, she looks at the article as a whole, what the message is she wants to impart and then breaks it down into smaller sections or paragraphs, sometimes even starting by writing the end statement. Having got something down, her brain then relaxes into a more creative writing mode and she's off, crafting another excellent piece.

If that doesn't help, perhaps you can decide to stop trying and do something else instead. While it may seem as though procrastination has won the day, sometimes trying too hard just stops you dead in the water. So doing *something*, even if it is an unrelated task, can sometimes be the relief valve your brain is looking for.

2. Understand what is being asked of you

It is much easier to get on with a new task when you know with absolute certainty exactly what is being asked of you. Also, you are less likely to procrastinate over a familiar task.

Your brain loves *certainty* and patterns it can recognise. Having that certainty diminishes the brain's stress response. So if you are not sure you completely understand the job that needs to be done, ask for clarification whenever possible. It could save you a whole heap of time and more.

Nick had started a new job, which he was very excited about. He felt confident he would be able to work well in his new role. The first task he was given, however, was something he hadn't had much experience of, even though he knew he should be able to give it a good shot. His unease around feeling unsure of what was really being asked of him and his fear of "doing it wrong" stopped him in his tracks.

Later on in his first day, when his boss asked how he was going, Nick came up with a couple of lame excuses for why he hadn't started, and his boss got angry with him.

This scenario could have easily been avoided if:

    (a) Nick had sought clarification about what the task was really all about and how his boss wanted it done

    (b) Nick's boss had checked with his new staff member to

ensure he did have that certainty around the task and what was being asked of him.

It's not always that we don't know how to do a piece of work. It could be the uncertainty of the policies, procedures, and protocols associated with the work that cause the uncertainty.

- Does your workplace provide certainty for all its members? If not, what are some of the ways that this could be provided?
- Does it require the managers to review how assignments and tasks are allocated and explained?
- Does it require improved communication channels between the different parties?
- Does it require a better "checking in" system for monitoring performance?

PROCRASTINATION AND SEEING THINGS THROUGH

Maybe getting started isn't what holds you back. Could the problem be persevering for long enough to get through all the work required? Because let's face it, not everything we have to do is scintillatingly exciting. Sometimes the excitement is with starting the new project, implementing a new strategy, or just coming up with great new ideas.

Sticking with all the associated work can be tricky. It's like long-distance flying: the interesting parts are the take-off and landing; sitting on your bottom in cramped conditions for many hours can quickly become tedious, even when you know that ultimately the

PERSEVERING WITH A TASK CAN BE TRICKY: LIKE COPING WITH LONG DISTANCE FLYING.

journey will bring you to your desired destination. This is where having sufficient motivation is critical.

Dr Jason Fox is a leading expert in motivation design and the structures that inspire great work. Jason shows organisations how to use the science of motivation with game design to shift behaviour and shape culture. His expertise incorporates the idea that the biggest motivator to reach our goals is not simply visualising the outcome or setting ourselves SMART goals. It is about the *progress* we see we have made. (Yes, you do have to do the work first, but you knew that, didn't you?). Reviewing progress requires you to pause from time to time and look back to see just how far you have come. It's like looking at the flight tracker on your inflight screen to see how far you have already travelled — and anticipating the warm reception you'll get at your destination.

Now, your reward for progress doesn't have to be an expensive, super-huge wristwatch, after all this is just rewarding your progress. The big reward comes later at the end. For now it's about finding the right-sized reward that will make you feel good enough to want to continue, because then you get to complete and get the big prize at the end, and *that* is what makes you and your brain feel really good.

What could these rewards be? Well, they just need to be things that you like and will enjoy — and, yes, it can be a bit more than just an extra cup of coffee.

Jason points out that research has revealed a mismatch between what managers believe motivates staff and what the staff really think. If your managers are still of the thinking that bonuses and financial rewards are what matter, they are sadly working in the wrong era. It is our sense of progress and the feeling we are doing meaningful work that are of most value to us, and of course to our business or organisation as well.

Sarah prided herself on being an ideas girl. There was nothing she loved more than allowing her brain to run free and come up with great and innovative ideas. The problem was that she was inept at seeing them through, often leaving a trail of frustration and broken dreams behind her. The task of implementing the work needed to bring her ideas to life bored her. Being a solopreneur, she realised the only way to move forward was to find a way to complete a task before getting side-tracked onto the next bright shiny idea. She enlisted a business coach who worked with her over several months, providing a framework that allowed her to plot her progress with her current projects, and to ensure she made the necessary stops along the way to reflect on her progress and enjoy mini rewards, such as taking an afternoon off for a massage or facial, or for coffee with a girlfriend.

If your problem is in persevering with the task at hand, it's time to set yourself a series of mini targets that allow you to mark your progress and enjoy the rewards along the way.

FINISHING OFF

The question is, "Do you complete?"

To buy a new garment, get it home, and realise that one of the seams is already coming undone because it wasn't finished properly is annoying as well as disappointing. Finishing off can be a big obstacle for many people who love the thrill of starting new projects and getting them going, but have lost interest by the time it comes to the finish. These are often the people who have multiple projects underway. Their forte is coming up with a new idea, but once it is established they are distracted by the next bright idea or concept — and away they go, leaving a trail of unfinished work.

Finishing off can also be a challenge in a world that requires us to divert our attention to multiple projects. Which is why many households with do-it-yourselfers live too long with unfinished renovations – the last wall that needed repainting, or those cupboards that are just waiting for their new handles to be attached. It's also why those hobbies: car restorations, making a digital album of last year's holiday snaps, or finishing the quilt for your best friend's baby, keep being put off.

Yet failing to complete that last little piece (often just the last 5% of the project) can ultimately cost you your chance for higher achievement. How many of us sabotage our own success by simply failing to complete the job, just like the two people on my Post Graduate Course?

Ask any athlete if they would ever consider pulling up just before the finish line and they are likely to consider you quite mad. Have you ever had to do a 5000-piece jigsaw puzzle, only to realise that you are one piece short at the end?

So are there some ways to help you finish your work, every time?

1. **Be accountable.** This might be to yourself, your team, or an accountability buddy.
   You specify the completion date and how it will be completed, and you check in when it's done.
2. **Prioritise your tasks.** Do not allow yourself the feel-good of starting something new until you have finished the work in hand.
3. **Acknowledge completion and reward yourself.**
   Okay, this is when the big prize comes in handy. Instead of dashing off to the next project or piece of work, stop!

This is the time to acknowledge to yourself that, yes, you have completed. Yes, you did hand in the assignment on time. Yes, you did complete the workbook. Yes, you did finish reading that set of documents.

Now is the time to share your good news. Share your success with your friends, family, or whoever will listen. It's also great to share in another person's success, and the positive emotion generated will inspire you to succeed.

THE VALUE OF DEADLINES

Deadlines are ubiquitous, or so it seems. The thought of yet another deadline to meet fills some people with dread. For others, though, the deadline is just a line in the sand, an indicator of where you have to be at a certain time and place. Appropriately managed deadlines can be very useful, especially for people who recognise their procrastinating tendencies and want to overcome them.

In his book *Predictably Irrational*, behavioural economist Dan Ariely[62] describes a study he did in 2002 with his colleague Klaus Wertenbrock. Dan is a brilliant raconteur and scientist who studies that curious phenomenon called human behaviour. In this study he was examining how students procrastinate over handing in their assignments. My fellow students might have benefited from reading his book!

Even if you have never studied at university, I'm sure you will remember from schooldays how the teacher would hand out assignments and projects along with their specified completion dates. Do you remember that horror of spending two sleepless nights before the Monday morning deadline feverishly trying to get all the work done? Yep, me too.

In this experiment, three different classes studying the same subject were allocated three assignments. The only difference between the classes was in their instructions for submission.

- **Class A** were asked to submit all three assignments on the last day of classes.
- **Class B** were asked to define and state their own schedule of deadlines.
- **Class C** were required to submit the three papers, one at a time, at a fixed, evenly spaced deadline over the three week period.

The question was, which class would receive the best average grades? The answer may not surprise you. It was Class C that did best. Being given a specific deadline by someone else works best for reducing procrastination and maximising performance. Spacing out the assignment deadlines is also what makes the difference.

The second best form of deadline is the one we make for ourselves, so Class B didn't do too badly. It's just harder sometimes to remain accountable to ourselves rather than to someone else.

Class A did what most of us tend to do: they put the work off until the last week, when the reality of the impending deadline really started to bite, and then of course they had not just one but all three papers to complete.

Professor Ariely's findings revealed that if we recognise our tendency to procrastinate, being provided a tool, such as how to precommit to a deadline, is what can help us to the outcomes we are looking to achieve.

Why do we do this? It's because we fall foul of what is known as the *planning fallacy*.

IT'S NOT ABOUT FAILING TO PLAN

I'm sure you will have heard the saying "If you fail to plan, you plan to fail". Nice idea, but actually not terribly helpful to procrastinators like you and me. It's not that we fail to plan. It's just that we are notoriously bad at estimating how long a particular task will take. Our tendency is to underestimate what we can achieve in a short time frame while overestimating what we can achieve in the longer term.

Which is why when scheduling work in your timetable you may allocate three tasks to be completed before lunch, but find yourself still working through the second item at 3 pm. It's also why we start our three-week project thinking we will have nailed it well within the allocated time, but actually achieve very little in the first or second week. Have you ever had that experience where the task you are doing simply expands to fill all the time available?

It comes down to understanding that the present and the future are two different concepts. Brilliant thinking, Sherlock. It's the way your brain considers these differences that is important. The here and now is real to your brain. It is concrete, a fact, and you are living it. The future, on the other hand, is abstract and your brain doesn't manage abstract thought very well. It much prefers the certainty of the here and now, which it can compare and contrast to your previous knowledge and experience. Abstract thought is stressful to your brain and you may remember that what the brain finds stressful has an impact on your ability to think.

This is where the power of visualisation comes in handy. If you can picture yourself as having *already* achieved your goal or handed in your assignment, it is treated by the brain as a given because you have now transformed it into a reality, a concrete construct that is of no threat to your brain.

Athletes and others have used this to help them achieve success. Michael Jordan, as already mentioned, is well known for visualising himself playing a basketball game. Others visualise themselves winning a race or tournament, and afterwards standing on the podium to collect the gold medal. It helps to overcome all the "what ifs" and quietens down the negative chatter in our brain so it can concentrate on what needs to be done.

Belinda is very organised and efficient. She likes to start on new projects immediately so as to allow herself sufficient time to get the work done, as she hates finishing in a rush. Ted is a bit of a slacker, but is highly motivated to ensure that he does okay and that his boss thinks he is just plain wonderful. Eric isn't really that fussed. He knows he tends to put things off, but then he usually comes good when the pressure is on to produce the required outcome.

So who produces the best work? I'd like to tell you it's Belinda, because she is like me, "Miss Plodalong", slow and steady, working hard and ensuring the work is completed adequately and (mostly) on time. It isn't Eric, who as usual procrastinates over getting going, then at the last minute pulls an all-nighter and hands in the work, just a tad late. It's not his best effort, but at least he got it done.

It's Ted who, despite also procrastinating, has the motivation and willpower to pull out all the stops at the end, working really hard and gliding across the finish line with some really cool ideas.

So the fable of the tortoise and the hare is only partly true. If you are a hare who is highly motivated and ambitious, the race can still be yours. If you are a hare who maintains the self-delusion that good enough will necessarily get you to your destination, then you are likely to have a string of "seconds" to your name.

I used to know quite a few Teds at university and they would drive me mad. There was nothing worse than slaving away for weeks to get an okay mark and then seeing "Ted", who sat next to you in lectures when he could be bothered to show up, who borrowed your notes and did little work until the very last moment, come out top of the class. Grrr!

Ahh, such is life. There will always be the Teds, Erics and Belindas. While the Belindas may procrastinate less about starting, the statistics reveal that in the end we all mostly get done what needs to be done. Though if you are an Eric, you are seriously at risk of underperforming and never achieving your full potential.

Procrastination can sometimes make me feel slightly schizophrenic. I will often set myself tasks to complete, which I know will assist me in building my business. I then systematically go about sabotaging my own efforts to achieve them.

An example would be failing to follow up after doing some work for a client, to see if there is anything else I can offer that would be of value to them. Common sense would say of course you should do this, yet even with self-imposed deadlines and schedules and task sheets, sometimes the follow-up gets delayed, and ultimately deferred indefinitely.

Why?

Daniel McRaney[63], author of *You Are Not So Smart*, sums it up nicely. When it comes to goal setting, we are basically two different people: "Now You" and "Future You". The trouble is, "Future You" cannot be trusted! My goal is to follow up with my pre-existing clients and I plan to do so in the future, but my future plan may not match how I actually feel or think when the time eventually arrives. So it becomes easier to adopt the route of avoidance of a task I find difficult.

Think of all the people in the world who are struggling with their weight and would dearly love to drop a few kilos. Have you ever wanted to lose weight? Perhaps you have mapped out how much and in what time frame, which of course falls into future planning. Yet when dinnertime comes around and you have had a stressful and tiring day, and you are starving because you missed lunch (feeling very virtuous at the time), all you want to do is to plop down in front of the telly with a large glass of wine and a takeaway. The battle between "Now You" and "Future You" is a one-sided contest every time.

Our future can be big, bold . . . and often somewhat fuzzy. We may think our life will be perfect if only we win the Lottery, but how many stories have you heard of people who did win, only to lose it all in a relatively short period of time?

We suffer from what is called *Present Bias*. We believe that our future happiness depends on a particular prospective event, such as getting that promotion or pay rise, and yet when we get it, we discover that it isn't all we'd expected. There are conditions, a down side. Perhaps your responsibility suddenly escalates way beyond your comfort zone, or that pay rise is quickly gobbled up by higher costs elsewhere.

WOULD YOU LIKE TO LOOK AT THE DESSERT MENU?

My husband always smiles when he hears that line when we are out for dinner, because he knows what my response will be. "No thanks, I'm really much too full. Just a cup of peppermint tea, please." The smile is because he knows that if he orders dessert, I will usually end up eating half of it!

Temptation, though, is time sensitive and here procrastination can be used to your *advantage*.

Simple suppression of your thoughts doesn't work. I'm sure you'll be familiar with the thought experiment in which you are asked to think about a pink elephant and nothing but the pink elephant.

Having visualised this pink elephant and had it firmly in front of your mind for a minute or two, you are now asked to think of a green giraffe but, whatever you do, don't think about the elephant.

What happens? You think about the elephant, because your mind was primed to think that thought first. The very act of suppressing a thought brings it to your consciousness, so any effort *not* to think about it is destined to fail.

Have you ever had a time when you are being very good at saying no to something, and then your willpower completely breaks down and you succumb?

Your thoughts may have moved to past efforts to resist chocolate, but what about those times at work? You have an important document that simply *has* to be completed for your boss by early afternoon, but the rest of your team are going down to your favourite sushi bar for lunch?

Delaying your decision here is key to resolving the issue. You may need lunch, but shooting off to the sushi bar is going to cost too much precious time to get your work done. A response of "Give me ten minutes and I'll see if I can" gives you the time you need to overcome that first impulse of "Let's go!" After ten minutes, the urgency and immediacy of the idea has passed and it's much easier to come to a decision that may serve you better.

This technique can be used in exactly the same way with the dessert menu. If I can delay my husband ordering for ten minutes by asking the waitress, "Can you bring the menu over in a few minutes", he is less likely to order anything because the temptation has lessened, and I am less likely to end up eating half a dessert I didn't need or really want!

The closer a temptation is to us, the bigger the effect on our ability to procrastinate. So turn it around and use those delaying tactics to serve you better! This is where you can become a modern-day Ulysses, capable of warding off the temptation of singing Sirens (or dessert!) by first recognising the danger and then shielding yourself somehow from the lurking temptation.

TAMING THE BEAST OF PROCRASTINATION

Procrastination is an expensive behaviour to indulge in because it costs us time, energy, and potential success. So if it is a behaviour you would like to see better managed, there are a number of strategies you can adopt to help you tame your own beast.

1. **First up, admit to it!** There's nothing like confessing to a trait that you want to be rid of.

2. **Identify what is causing you to procrastinate.** Are you a person who can't get started because [. . .] or who can't maintain the momentum because [. . .] or who does 95% of the work but can never quite complete it because [. . .]?

3. **Start now!** Choose one strategy to help you overcome your main issue and put it into practice.

4. **Some tasks are boring but still have to be done.** Finding a way to increase the value of the task will help to lower your risk of procrastination. Filing may not get you very excited, but look at it as a way of helping the business to function better. Reframing the task moves your brain into a "towards" state that is looking to receive a reward, which is far more motivating than denying yourself something as a stepping-stone to a bigger goal, such as getting accredited in your field of expertise, or getting promoted.

5. **Prioritise.** Choose which two or three tasks absolutely must get done and then choose the most important one to do first. Brian Tracey talks about choosing your three frogs (tasks) and always eating the biggest, ugliest one first.

6. **Recognise your distractions** and then find a way to

circumvent their effect. If having people knocking on your door is a problem, how about closing the door with an old-fashioned "Do not disturb — brain at work" sign?

7. **Resist your temptations through distance.** If you can't resist walking past the cookie jar for another biscuit in the office kitchen, get your coffee elsewhere or put the jar somewhere else, though maybe you should tell your colleagues what you are doing and why, first!

8. **Work out your plan,** and then plan for contingencies. Maintaining a level of flexibility with all tasks ensures that you can keep moving forward. Goals are useful but they don't have to be set in concrete, because situations and expectations change. Knowing you can adjust your goal to keep it relevant and appropriate to your needs is what matters.

9. **Understand what is being asked of you.** Providing your brain with certainty will give you confidence in your ability to do the work and elevate your performance.

10. **Avoid overwhelm.** Too much to do and unsure where to start? This is where overwhelm can sneak in, creating anxiety and leading to poorer decision-making. After prioritising, break down the tasks into smaller challenges. Practise being mindful to notice how you are feeling and reacting to a situation. Acknowledging the emotion helps to calm down your brain, allowing you to work out the best place to start.

11. **Afraid of failure?** Not many people enjoy failing at things. Our education system encourages us to always strive hard, to do our best, to pass all of our exams. Passing exams is

a measure of our academic success, yet failure can be an extraordinary learning tool. If you can embrace failure as a possible outcome, you can eliminate the fear that is holding you back from giving your goal a go. You may experience greater regret from not trying something than from giving it a go and failing. If you fail, fail well, fail fast, and simply move on to the next item. Michael Jordan attributes his phenomenal success to all of his failures.

12. **Persevere.** Find whatever supports you to maintain a sense of progress and motivation, and moves you towards the finish line.

13. **Finish off.** If you are sabotaging your own success by not completing that last 5%, add a deadline, plan a reward (big enough that you really want it) and commit to not starting anything else *until* this current project or task is signed off.

14. **Choose not to procrastinate!** It is a behaviour, one that can be tamed and modified, but it requires your decision and commitment to make it happen. Make that choice with a really big WHY you want to change.

15. **Surround yourself with others who will support you on your journey.** When I ask successful business people what has contributed to their success, they may mention the hard work and their commitment to the process, but invariably they will say it is the support, input, and accountability provided by a coach or mentor. Do you have a support person? Our mentors will often appear at different times in our lives and we usually have more than one.

Piers Steel talks about creating an upward spiral of success that can be achieved through accomplishing more. A higher level of accomplishment creates greater confidence and the more confidence you enjoy, the more effort you may be willing to exert, which leads to greater accomplishment. It seems common sense, but are you applying it?

By practising and succeeding in overcoming your procrastinating tendencies, you set yourself up for future success by rewiring your brain and forming healthy non-procrastinating brain habits.

If you think you need some extra support, there is help available. Procrastinators Anonymous is a website where you can find others like yourself, and share experiences and tools to help overcome your procrastinating habits.

CHAPTER 6

BUILDING BRAIN SMARTNESS

Brain Smart was written to provide insight and understanding around some of the challenges many of us are facing today. It won't necessarily provide you with all the answers, however my purpose was to start you thinking around some of the issues you may be facing, so you can start to put some techniques and strategies into place to produce positive change.

Elevating mental performance through smarter thinking has to start with brain fitness first. Once you have optimised your brain's health and function, you are now ready to effectively polish up your thinking skills and mental capability.

Brain fitness (just like physical fitness) is achieved by training your brain. Because your brain is "plastic" this means it is continually rewiring itself in response to new stimuli it receives from our environment. Neuroplasticity is a normal function of the brain that you can use to enhance your mental agility and flexibility in just the same way as you might choose to improve your cardiovascular fitness. You can choose to improve your mental "muscles" such as attention, willpower, and memory.

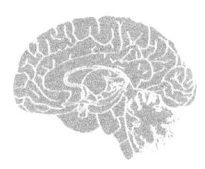

BRAIN FITNESS (JUST LIKE PHYSICAL FITNESS) IS ACHIEVED BY TRAINING YOUR BRAIN: HARNESSING YOUR BRAIN'S NATURAL PLASTICITY TO REWIRE AND UPSKILL YOUR THINKING.

Once you have improved your thinking skills, by continuing the appropriate practice on an ongoing basis you can continue to enjoy the benefits of smarter thinking.

Chronic severe stress and depression are highly damaging to our thinking skills, being associated with physiological loss of volume in our hippocampus, the area of the brain essential for learning and memory encoding. Recognising the danger signs of too much stress or a potential mental illness is critical to help minimise the potential damage to thinking and memory.

Our attention skills provided us with an essential survival tool. However, our current lifestyle in many instances is contributing to an erosion of our attention span. If this is not addressed, it has the potential to make keeping up with the continuing rapid introduction of new technologies much harder. Introducing strategies in our lives and in the workplace to enhance our focus will enable us all to adapt more easily to retain our intellect and cognitive agility.

Like any good working relationship, it will be through working with our brain, by understanding how it best likes to work, and recognising its limitations, that we will elevate our true mental capability and reap the benefits of higher mental performance.

As Edward de Bono said, "An expert is someone who has succeeded in making decisions and judgements simpler through knowing what to pay attention to and what to ignore." We do not need to be experts for this to be a truth that applies to us all.

AFTERWORD: LIVING WITH A SMARTER BRAIN

We are living in extraordinary times. Our world may appear frantic and chaotic, even overwhelming, yet we are also witnessing the birth of new technologies and change at a pace never previously witnessed. We are gathering knowledge and understanding of areas previously unexplored, and harnessing this to our brain's advantage as we move towards the future.

Smarter thinking enables us to enhance our brain's capability. We build a higher level of mental performance through our awareness of how our brain works best and implementing that knowledge in a useful way: focusing attention, managing distractions, and recognising our own brain's limitations.

Our brain's function and improvement is a continuum. Moving from a fit brain that is optimised to be healthy, to a smart brain that has greater capacity, raises prospects of how to effectively embrace change and innovation using not only our emotional intelligence, but our social intelligence skills too. Then we can start to look towards greater collaboration and contribution, the essence of leadership of ourselves and of others, which is the subject of the next book in this series: *Brain Change*.

I look forward to meeting you there.

REFERENCES

[1] Howard Gardner (2008). *Five Minds for the Future.* Boston: Harvard Business Press.

[2] Dr Jenny Brockis (2011). *Brain Fit! How smarter thinking can save your brain.* Marri Press.

[3] Gary Small and Gigi Vorgan (2008). *iBrain: Surviving the technological alteration of the modern mind.* New York: HarperCollins.

[4] www.blackdoginstitute.org.au

[5] Medibank, KPMG Econtech (July 2011). *Sick at Work: The cost of presenteeism to your business and the economy.*

[6] John Medina (2009). *Brain Rules: Twelve principles for surviving and thriving at work, home and school.* Seattle, US: Pear Press.

[7] Amy Arnsten (2009). *The Emerging Neurobiology of Attention Deficit Hyperactivity Disorder: The Key Role of the Prefrontal Association Cortex. Journal of Pediatrics.* 1 May, 154(5): I–S43. DOI: 10.1016/j.jpeds.2009.01.018

[8] Torkel Klingberg (2010). Training and plasticity of working memory. *Trends in Cognitive Sciences* 14: 317–24. DOI: 10.1016/j.tics.2010.05.002

[9] Dr Mark Katz. SALT Center, University of Arizona.

[10] R.L. Buckner, J.R. Andrews-Hanna and D.L. Schacter (2008). The brain's default network: anatomy, function, and relevance to disease. *Annals of the New York Academy of Sciences.* March, 1124: 1–38. DOI: 10.1196/annals.1440.011

[11] Daniel Goleman (1995). *Emotional Intelligence: Why it can matter more than I.Q.* New York: Bantam Books.

[12] Evian Gordon (Ed.) (2000). NeuroLeadership and Integrative Neuroscience: "it's about validation stupid!" *NeuroLeadership Journal, 2008.*

[13] Too much screen time is bad for thinkitng brains. http://www.aap.org/en-us/advocacy-and-policy/aap-health-initiatives/Pages/Media-and-Children

[14] Betsy Sparrow, Jenny Liu and Daniel M. Wegner (2011). Google effects on memory: Cognitive consequences of having information at our fingertips. *Science.* 14 July. DOI: 10.1126/science.1207745

[15] Eleanor A. Maguire, David G. Gadian, Ingrid S. Johnsrude, Catriona D. Good, John Ashburner, Richard S.J. Frackowiak and Christopher D. Frith (2000). Navigation-related structural change in the hippocampi of taxi drivers. *Proceedings of the National Academy of Sciences* 97(8): 4398–4403.

[16] D.O. Hebb (1949). *The Organisation of Behaviour.* New York: John Wiley & Sons.

[17] A. Pascual-Leone, D. Nguyet, L.G. Cohen, J.P. Brasil-Neto, A. Cammarota, and M. Hallett (1995). Modulation of muscle responses evoked by transcranial magnetic stimulation during the acquisition of new fine motor skills. American Physiological Society. *Journal of Neurophysiology* 74(3): 1037–45.

[18] Margaret C. McKinnon, Kaan Yucel, Anthony Nazarov and Glenda M. MacQueen (2009). A meta-analysis examining clinical predictors of hippocampal volume in patients with major depressive disorder. *Journal of Psychiatry and Neuroscience.* January, 34(1): 41–54.

[19] I. Hickie et al. (2005). Reduced hippocampal volumes and memory loss in patients with early- and late-onset depression. *British Journal of Psychiatry.* March, 186: 197–202.

[20] N. Schuff et al. (2009). Alzheimer's Disease Neuroimaging Initiative. MRI of hippocampal volume loss in early Alzheimer's disease in relation to ApoE genotype and biomarkers. *Brain.* April, 132(4): 1067–77. DOI: 10.1093/brain/awp007

[21] Lila Davachi, Tobias Kiefer, David Rock and Lisa Rock (2010). Learning that lasts through AGES. *Neuroleadership Journal,* issue 3.

[22] David M. Sanbonmatsu, David L. Strayer, Nathan Medeiros-Ward and Jason M. Watson (2013). Who multi-tasks and why? Multi-tasking ability, perceived multi-tasking ability, impulsivity, and sensation seeking. *PLoS ONE,* 8(1): e54402. DOI: 10.1371/journal.pone.0054402

[23] D.R. Godden and A.D. Baddeley (1975). Context-dependent memory in two natural environments: on land and underwater. *British Journal of Psychology,* 66(3): 325–31.

[24] http://www.fastcompany.com/3005011/why-you-should-work-coffee-shop-even-when-you-have-office?partner=newsletter

[25] David Marks (1973). Visual Imagery Difference in the recall of pictures. *British Journal of Psychology.* February, 64(1): 17–24.

[26] Michael. I. Posner and Steven E Petersen (1990). The attention system of the human brain. *Annual Reviews of Neuroscience,* 13: 25–42.

[27] Jeffrey Schwartz (2012). *You Are Not Your Brain: The four step solution for changing bad habits, ending unhealthy thinking, and taking control of your life.* New York: Penguin.

[28] Gerald Olivero, K. Denise Bane and Richard E. Kopelman (1997). Executive coaching as a transfer of training tool: Effects on productivity in a public agency. *Public Personnel Management* 26(4) (Winter). Research on the value of follow-up in coaching.

[29] Kristen Hansen, Enhansen performance.com.au

[30] Giannotti D, Patrizi G, Di Rocco G, Vestri AR, Semproni CP, et al. (2013) Play to Become a Surgeon: Impact of Nintendo WII Training on Laparoscopic Skills. *PLoS ONE* 8(2): e57372. doi:10.1371/journal.pone.0057372

[31] Mihaly Csikszentmihalyi (2008). *Flow: The Psychology of Optimal Experience*. New York: Harper & Row.

[32] Christopher Chabris and Daniel Simons (2010). *The Invisible Gorilla: How our intuitions deceive us*. New York: Broadway, Random House.

[33] Pearls before Breakfast, Washington Post. (2007) http://www.washingtonpost.com/wp-dyn/content/article/2007/04/04/AR2007040401721.html

[34] Ed Hallowell (2005). Overloaded circuits: Why smart people underperform. *Harvard Business Review* January 2005

[35] Matt Liebermann et al. (2007). Putting feelings into words: Affect labelling disrupts amygdala. *Psychological Science* 18(5): 421–28.

[36] Jon Kabat-Zinn (1991). *Full Catastrophe Living: Using the wisdom of your body and mind to face stress, pain, and illness*. Delta. ISBN 0-385-30312-2.

[37] Britta K. Hölzel, James Carmody, Mark Vangel, Christina Congleton, Sita M. Yerramsetti, Tim Gard and Sara W. Lazar (2011). Mindfulness practice leads to increases in regional brain gray matter density. *Psychiatry Research: Neuroimaging* 191(1): 36. DOI: 10.1016/j.pscychresns.2010.08.006

[38] Carol Dweck (2007). *Mindset: The new psychology of success*. New York: Ballantine Books.

[39] Erik M. Altmann, J Gregory Trafton and David Z. Hambrick (2013). Momentary Interruptions Can Derail the Train of Thought. *Journal of Experimental Psychology: General.* 7 January. DOI: 10.1037/a0030986

[40] Laura Dabbish, Gloria Mark and Víctor M. González (2011). Why do I keep interrupting myself?: Environment, habit and self-interruption. In *Proceedings of the SIGCHI Conference on Human Factors in Computing Systems* (CHI '11). ACM, New York, 3127–30. DOI: 10.1145/1978942.1979405

[41] Matthew Killingsworth and Daniel Gilbert (2010). A wandering mind is an unhappy mind. *Science.* 12 November 330: 932. DOI: 10.1126/science.1192439

[42] J. Bohannon (2011). Searching for the Google effect on memory. *Science*, July, 333(15): 277.

[43] Zheng Wang and John M. Tchernev (2012). The "myth" of media multitasking: Reciprocal dynamics of media multitasking, personal needs, and gratifications. *Journal of Communication.* DOI: 10.1111/j.1460-2466.2012.01641.x

[44] Sylvain Charron and Etienne Koechlin (2010). Divided Representation of Concurrent Goals in the Human Frontal Lobes. *Science*, 16 April, 328(5976): 360–63. DOI: 10.1126/science.1183614

[45] Eyal Ophir, Clifford Nass and Anthony D. Wagner (2009). Cognitive control in media multitaskers. *Proceedings of the National Academy of Sciences* 106(37): 15583–87. DOI: 10.1073/pnas.0903620106

[46] http://www.telegraph.co.uk/motoring/news/6252919/Half-a-million-road-crashes-caused-by-women-drivers-applying-make-up.html

[47] Amy N. Ship (2010). The most primary of care — talking about driving and distraction.
New England Journal of Medicine 362(23): 2145–47.

[48] Gloria Mark, Victor M. Gonzalez and Justin Harris (2005). No task left behind?: Examining the nature of fragmented work. In *Proceedings of the SIGCHI Conference on Human Factors in Computing Systems* (CHI '05). ACM. New York, 321–30. DOI: 10.1145/1054972.1055017

[49] Gloria Mark, Stephen Voida and Armand Cardello (2012). A pace not dictated by electrons: An empirical study of work without email. Department of Infomatics UCLA and US Army Natick Soldier RD&E Center.

[50] Jani Murphy, www.janimurphy.com

[51] Craig Smith, www.expandedramblings.com

[52] Wistia infographic (2011). http://wistia.com/blog/what-kinds-of-videos-do-americans-watch-at-work/

[53] Hideto Yuzawa and Gloria Mark (2010). The Japanese garden: Task awareness for collaborative multitasking. In *Proceedings of the 16th ACM international conference on supporting group work* (GROUP '10). ACM. New York, 253–62. DOI: 10.1145/1880071.1880114

[54] Paul E. Dux et al. (2009). Training improves multitasking performance by increasing the speed of information processing in human prefrontal cortex. *Neuron*. 16 July, 63(1): 127–38. DOI: 10.1016/j.neuron.2009.06.005

[55] Piers Steel (2010). *The Procrastination Equation*. New York: HarperCollins.

[56] Dr Jason Fox, Motivation Strategy and Design Expert, www.drjasonfox.com

[57] Walter Mischel, Yuichi Shoda, Monica L Rodriguez (1989). Delay of Gratification in Children. *Science, New Series*, Vol.244, No. 4907 p 933-938.

[58] B. J. Casey, L. H. Somerville, I.H. Gotlib, O. Ayduk, N.T. Franklin, M.K. Askren, J. Jonides, M. G. Berman, N. L. Wilson, T. Teslovich, G. Glover, V. Zayas, W. Mischel and Y. Shoda (2011). Behavioral and neural correlates of delay of gratification 40 years later. *Proceedings of the National Academy of Sciences.* DOI: 10.1073/pnas.1108561108

[59] Martin Seligman (2012). *Flourish: A visionary new understanding of happiness and well-being.* New York: Simon and Schuster.

[60] Roy F. Baumeister and John Tierney (2012). *Willpower: Rediscovering the greatest human strength.* New York: Penguin.

[61] Barry Schwartz (2005). *The Paradox of Choice: Why more is less.* New York: HarperCollins.

[62] Dan Ariely (2008). *Predictably Irrational.* New York: HarperCollins.

[63] Daniel McRaney (2012). *You Are Not So Smart.* New York: Penguin.

ABOUT THE AUTHOR

Dr Jenny Brockis is passionate about helping individuals and organisations achieve their best outcomes through better brain health and function. She is an educator, mentor, author, and award-winning speaker. She seeks to inspire greater performance by simplifying the complexity of the brain science into practical applications that are relevant to everyday life. Her mission is to make brain fitness as much a part of our culture as physical fitness.

A lifelong learner, she is a qualified "Nightingale" nurse from St. Thomas' Hospital, a medical practitioner holding an MB ChB (Brist) and Fellowship of the Royal Australian College of General Practitioners (WA) and has completed a postgraduate certificate in the Neuroscience of Leadership.

Today Jenny works with companies, business leaders and educators, sharing her knowledge and expertise to inspire, motivate and activate the brains of others. When not delivering keynote presentations, workshops, or mentoring, she is researching the latest findings from neuroscience, and writing articles, books, and her blog.

Happily married with two young adult children, Jenny lives in beautiful Perth, Western Australia, with two border terriers and one dog-weary cat. She loves to spend time with family and friends, enjoys travel, exploring Australia's rugged Outback and snow skiing (although there's never enough snow in Western Australia), and is addicted to books and learning.

Her popular book *Brain Fit!* is now in its second edition. *Brain Smart* is the second book in the series.

To find out more, get in touch or sign up to her blog, visit www.drjennybrockis.com

www.ingramcontent.com/pod-product-compliance
Lightning Source LLC
Chambersburg PA
CBHW050906160426
43194CB00011B/2314